Socialization
after Childhood:
Two Essays

Socialization after Childhood: Two Essays

ORVILLE G. BRIM, Jr.
STANTON WHEELER

John Wiley & Sons, Inc.
New York   London   Sydney

Preface

The two essays which comprise this volume are designed to reflect recent contributions to the study of socialization after childhood and to discuss some of the problems and concepts that appear to provide strategic points of entry for further developments in this field. The emphasis is on the impact of social forces and processes on personal development. But within this general framework, the two works are designed to fulfill somewhat different purposes.

The first essay provides an orienting perspective on many of the problems posed by the study of socialization through the life cycle. These include discussion of both the need for socialization after childhood and the limits to later-life socialization, the possible changes in the content of socialization as one moves through the life cycle, the effect of differing relationships between the socializing agent and the person being socialized, and some problems posed by the failure of socialization and the development of deviant behavior. The first essay, then, is designed to provide a broad overview of the topic.

The second is devoted to an examination of an increasingly important setting within which socialization after childhood occurs: the large-scale bureaucratic organization. This esssay describes some of the qualities of socializing organizations, especially those characteristics that may lead to differences in socialization outcomes. The specific focus is on the organizational qualities of schools, prisons, mental hospitals, and other organizations that process people.

Both essays are revisions of papers originally prepared for a conference under the title "Socialization through the Life Cycle," sponsored by the Social Science Research Council Committee on Socialization and Social Structure and held in New York, May 17–19, 1963. The participants in the conference were social scientists who were studying socialization in the different roles in social institutions from childhood to old age. The members of the Council's Committee on Socialization are John A. Clausen (chairman), Orville G. Brim, Jr., Alex Inkeles, Ronald Lippitt, Eleanor E. Maccoby, and M. Brewster Smith. The authors of papers presented at the conference were Howard S. Becker, Charles E. Bidwell, Irving Rosow, Murray A. Straus, and Yonina Talmon-Garber. The conference was supported by a grant made to the Social Science Research Council by the National Institute of Mental Health (Grant MY-04160).

Revision of the first essay benefited from the comments of the participants in the conference, and, as indicated in the text, several of the ideas presented emerged during the conference itself. The author wants to thank particularly Leonard S. Cottrell, Jr., Norman Goodman, and Theodore D. Kemper, his colleagues on several studies of personality and social structure, for their many contributions to the development of the ideas expressed, and Eleanor E. Maccoby and M. Brewster Smith for their critical evaluations of an earlier draft. Certain parts of this essay appeared in *Items*, a publication of the Social Science Research Council, in March 1964.

In its original form, the second essay served as a discussion of the paper presented at the conference by Howard S. Becker. That paper has since been published as "Personal Change in Adult Life," *Sociometry*, March 1964. Becker's paper served as a stimulus for many of the ideas presented in the original essay, and revisions of the paper have also profited from his helpful comments. In addition, the author of the second essay has profited greatly from the comments of members of the SSRC conference committee, and from critical readings of an earlier draft by Peter Blau, Blanche Geer, Eliot Freidson, Erving Goffman, and Arthur Stinchcombe.

ORVILLE G. BRIM, JR.
STANTON WHEELER

New York City
December, 1965

Contents

Socialization after Childhood

Socialization through the Life Cycle

ORVILLE G. BRIM, Jr.

SOCIALIZATION refers to the process by which persons acquire the knowledge, skills, and dispositions that make them more or less able members of their society. It is apparent that the socialization experienced by a person in childhood cannot prepare him for all the roles he will be expected to fill in later years. People move through a sequence of different positions in society, in accord with different stages of the life cycle. Changes in the demands upon them arise from their mobility, both geographic and social, and from the customs of their society which may vary during their lifetimes. A half century of important research on socialization of the child has described the development of children's personalities and social behavior; there has been much less work, almost none in comparison, on socialization at later stages of the life cycle. Moreover, neither those studying child socialization nor those studying adult socialization have yet realized the full extent of the similarity of their research interests, concepts, and procedures.

This essay is concerned with the characteristics of socialization at different times in the individual life span and is focused on the question of whether the fundamental components of socialization differ in important ways in different stages of the life cycle—in particular, whether there are differences between socialization in childhood and socialization in adulthood. Throughout, the objective has been to speculate, to try to identify topics warranting further study, and generally to open up the field of inquiry rather than to partition it into areas.

Personality in Relation to Society

There are two great traditions in the study of personality in relation to society. One is the interest in how individuals adjust to society and how in spite of the influence of society upon them they manage to be creative and gradually to transform the social order in which they have been born. The other is the interest in how society socializes the individual—how it transforms the raw material of biological man into a person suitable to perform the activities of society. The study of socialization falls into the latter tradition: its starting place is to ask the fundamental question of how it is possible for a society to endure and to continue to develop. The inquiry at all times is concerned with how society changes the natural man, not how man changes his society.

> An individual is prepared, with varying degrees of success, to meet the requirements laid down by other members of society for his behavior in a variety of situations. These requirements are always attached to one or another of the recognized positions or statuses in this society, such as husband, son, employee, and male adult. The behavior required of a person in a given position or status is considered to be the prescribed role, and the requirements themselves can be called "role prescriptions."
>
> The prescriptions for roles in any social system are directed to the successful discharge of the function of that system for society. Role prescriptions essentially are efforts on the part of society's members to regulate the behavior of other members so that certain consequences will follow. Role prescriptions, then, are based on theories, implicit or not, about human behavior. The prescriptions are for the behavior believed by society to be the instrumental means to the achievement of some desired result, that is, some specified function of the social system. It follows that changes in role prescriptions occur when the theories of human nature which underlie the prescriptions change, or when there is a change in the ends to be achieved by the social system. (7)

In simplest terms, the individual acquires the culture of his group(s) through socialization, which includes for our purposes two main divisions. One acquires an understanding of the recognized statuses—the traditional positions—in his society, learning the names so that he is able to locate other individuals in the social structure, as well as to identify himself. Not as much attention has been given to this aspect of the content of socialization; indeed, beyond the basic terms for age, sex, and a few others, we do not have any standard theoretical set of concepts that describe these positions. Secondly one learns, of course, role prescriptions and role behavior, with the associated modes of feeling. To summarize, the function of socialization is to transform the human raw material of society into good working members; the content can be considered analytically to include an understanding of the society's status structure and of the role prescriptions and behavior associated with the different positions in this structure.

In saying this, a few remarks are needed to avoid naïveté. A view of socialization as a process by which society creates persons suitable to carry out its functional requirements does not deny that sometimes the existing requirements of society are unrealistic and, according to one or another set of moral standards, unjust. Nor does it deny that sometimes the demands of society may limit, if not make impossible, the personal satisfactions of most of its members; or that the demands may be so irrational as to cause the disintegration of the society itself. Studies of the utility and of the morality of the demands of a given society upon its members are, of course, basic inquiries that go back as far as we have written records. This is not, however, the concern of the student of socialization. He asks how the work of society gets done and how the necessary manpower is trained, motivated, kept alive and functioning throughout the life cycle so that the specified roles are performed. His concern is not to understand how society is changed to fit man's nature better, or to improve his personal adjustment and satisfaction, but rather to understand how man is taught to get the work of society done. In the end, of course, what he learns from one line of inquiry pertains to the other. The analysis of socialization leads finally to the question of what is the desirable society.

Socialization into Social Roles

Our emphasis is on the acquisition of the habits, beliefs, attitudes, and motives which enable a person to perform satisfactorily the roles expected of him in his society. The acquisition of roles is not viewed as the entire content of socialization, but role learning is the segment of socialization that we propose to analyze, and role acquisition is probably the most important aspect of adult socialization.

Only recently has systematic attention been given in socialization studies to the acquisition of roles by children. Most work in the study of personality development has not had this specific phrasing of the problem or focus of interest. Although it has dealt with acquiring skills in social interaction, it has not concentrated on how an individual develops those organized, reciprocal, socially regulated interactions with other human beings which are role prescribed, or how he comes to distinguish between the important statuses in his society. Recently, Maccoby (21) has brought this question to the fore in child development research, and Sewell (27) has provided an up-to-date review of the few studies that have been made.

The emphasis in child development research, for several years after its beginning in the child welfare stations established soon after 1920, was more on maturation than socialization, more on development than learning. The major output has been studies of mental and physical development; only to a much lesser extent has there been research on the social and emotional aspects of development. The stimulus for much of the current work on socialization came from a different source: the work of Freud and related theories of personality. The effect of early-life experiences on the development of personality traits which were believed to be fundamental and enduring characteristics of the individual was the focus of study. It was later on, around 1930, that concepts emerging from cultural anthropology, especially the idea of cultural relativity and the plasticity of human nature, extended the scope of studies of personality and led to a convergence of the interests mentioned earlier. The traditional work on child development, combined with concepts stemming from clinical theories of personality and enhanced by cross-cultural perspectives, evolved into some notable studies of socialization. Even so, this work, for all of its contribution to our knowledge, did not concentrate on role learning as the content of socialization.

Throughout the history of child development research, the few studies which were being made of adult socialization—of personality change in later life, one might say—were different in their focus. They conceptualized socialization as learning new roles, and as the individual's adaptation to society's demands for changes in his social behavior as he moved from one position to the next. This is one of the most important reasons that convergence between child development research and adult socialization studies did not occur. Stating the problems involved in socialization as those of how social roles are learned may provide a focus for both child and adult studies and a meeting ground for those engaged in the two lines of research.

PERSONALITY VIEWED AS SELF-OTHER SYSTEMS

The Development of Self-Other Systems

The framework for the analysis of socialization through the life cycle needs to be sketched. It is more a point of view than a theory, and it is distinctively that of the sociologist. In much previous work in socialization (and personality theory generally) the sociologist's traditional concerns with role learning, social interaction, and the influence of reference groups have not been given much attention. This is understandable, considering the kinds of questions which have been asked in socialization studies, but when one turns to analyses of socialization at different periods in life, and especially later-life socialization, these concepts become highly valuable. One notes that these sociological ideas about personality are strictly limited to certain processes and components of personality; for example, they do not reflect much concern with cognitive processes or learning or the physiological bases of motivation. They can, however, be viewed as additional concepts and propositions about personality development and organization which eventually must be included in any comprehensive theory of personality.

It should be added that this view of personality reflects the societal approach to socialization, rather than the concern with problems of individual adjustment to the social order which are evident in most existing conceptions of personality. The historic assumption of conflict between the external social order and internal individual processes makes it difficult to be effective in the study of socialization. Personality processes have been analyzed with concepts which do not articulate with analyses of the outside social structure, and what is needed are personality concepts which permit easy and direct movement from characteristics of the social organization to its consequences for personality.* For example, if a man lives in a highly differentiated complex social structure, one can de-

* See Inkeles (15) for an analysis of this topic.

scribe the effects on his personality using the concept of heterogeneity of his significant reference figures. Similarly, where he is involved with persons who make conflicting and unresolvable role
demands, the concept of identity confusion permits one to move directly from the existence of conflict in the objective social order to
its consequences for personality.

The basic premise is that most of what is learned from socialization in childhood, and indeed throughout life, is a series of complex
interpersonal relationships. In the life of every person, there are a
number of people directly involved in socialization who have great
influence because of their frequency of contact, their primacy, and
their control over rewards and punishment. These persons, and the
expectations they have for the child's behavior, are of high salience
to him for continuing periods. Throughout the person's life these
people continue to influence the development of his character, even
as new significant persons are added, and the older ones displaced.
The result is the emergence of a series of "self-other systems," in
which the child is oriented toward the role prescriptions and evaluations of significant others in his environment.

Personality thus is constituted in large measure by learned interpersonal relationships, and in fact can be described and understood
in these terms. It follows that we should attempt to describe personality by reference to the individual's perceptions of himself and his
behavior, and of the social organization in which he lives. We
should be interested in the kinds of people he says are of greatest
significance to him, in what he thinks others expect him to do, and
in what they think about his performances. We should also know if
he accepts what others prescribe for him as right and legitimate, or
whether he thinks their expectations are unfair. We should know
much about his relationships, as he sees them, to the significant
others—whether he likes them, trusts them, thinks they are consistent in their behavior, whether the relationship is of long or short
duration, and so on. We should find out how he seeks to resolve conflicts between himself and others, and whether his attempts at resolution actually work or whether he continues in a state of conflicting
demands. All of these, and more, are significant components of his
personality and describe the important aspects of his relationships to
other people.

At this level of analysis we can say that the individual learns the behavior appropriate to his position in a group through interaction with others who hold normative beliefs about what his role should be, and who reward or punish him for correct or incorrect actions. Thus, common knowledge of others' expectations is indispensable in that the person must be able to predict how others will react to him to guide his own performance successfully. In the development of the individual's orientations toward the prescriptions of others for his behavior, it has been the important contribution of sociology to demonstrate that a major component of socialization involves learning the "role of the other," that is, trying to anticipate the other's response to one's own behavior, and reflecting upon one's own performance and appraising his behavior as good or bad. The expectations of others become symbolized, and their responses rehearsed symbolically. The paragraphs that follow are from an earlier theoretical statement which appeared in *Personality and Decision Processes* (9).

Mead views the self as a process by which the person can be both subject and object. That is, ego can act and he can consider his act as if he were an outsider looking at himself. The critical factor determining this reflexive character of the self-process is language. The important characteristic of language is that it provides a set of symbols having universal significance. The term "universal significance" means a symbol calls out the same response in ego that it calls out in alter. In short, universally significant symbols are shared. Thus, it is through the medium of significant communication that the individual is able to view himself in terms of the attitudes with which others view him. This formulation is extended to relate it to a concept of social role. Here Mead states that the attitudes of others incorporated as part of the self become systematically differentiated with regard to different alters.

Recent theoretical work also has been concerned with these problems in a more systematic manner. For example, Cottrell has drawn on Mead and others in an effort to derive a set of propositions for the systematic analysis of social interaction situations. . . . He uses two basic assumptions. First, he postulates that no item of social behavior can be viewed in isolation. Rather, it must be viewed in relation to its function as a part of a situation composed of other individuals. Second, he assumes that any person not only develops his own response patterns, but also incorporates the responses of the others (in the interactive system) in his own reactive system.

On the basis of these two assumptions, Cottrell then develops a set of formal propositions for the analysis of interpersonal behavior. One proposition states that after an interactive pattern (involving two persons) has been repeated a number of times, it becomes possible for each person to carry out covertly the entire pattern alone. . . .

One of Parsons' major interests has been the analysis of social interaction situations . . . . He postulates that in an interaction situation ego and alter serve as objects of orientation for one another. This premise is based upon the assumption that the outcome of ego's action (whether it is in some sense gratifying) is contingent upon alter's reaction to ego's behavior, since the latter's reaction can enhance or obstruct the movement of ego toward his goals. Consequently, ego becomes oriented to alter's expectations regarding ego's behavior. When interaction occurs over a period of time, this results in a tendency toward stability in the expectations of ego and alter and a consistent appropriateness of action and reaction. Such consistency tends to be maintained because each actor has some degree of control over rewards and punishments. Such orientation by ego and alter to the expectations of the other is reciprocal or complementary.

Parsons' analysis makes two things more explicit than they have been in the work of other theorists. First, he points out that it is the control over rewards and punishments which furnishes the motivation for ego and alter to become oriented to the expectations of one another. Second, he has made clear a distinction between mutual and complementary expectations. That is, in the stable interactive system the expectations of ego for alter and of alter for ego are complementary, whereas the expectations of ego for alter and of alter for himself are identical (mutual).

The major point emerging from the preceding discussion is that interaction results in the learning by ego of not only his own responses but also the responses of alters with whom he interacts. One implication of this is that ego should, under appropriate conditions, be able to reproduce alone the interaction pattern occurring between himself and alter.

Learning may take place through two other related processes. In the first process, there is a recognition by ego that alter is more successful than ego in some aspects of his behavior, and thus the appropriate elements of alter's behavior are consciously transferred to ego's role. We might call this a process of modeling or conscious imitation. Take . . . an . . . example in which a couple is trying to decide what to do about their child's disobedience, and the father is concerned primarily with the long-range consequences of various alternatives, while the mother is concerned mainly with the short-range consequences. The mother may recognize that the father's long-range concern leads to a course of action for dealing with the child that is superior to the way in which she has previously handled it. Consequently, she may decide to use the father's solution . . . .

In a related process, but one more complex than modeling, ego uses a trial-and-error approach to solving some problems for which his original responses have proved inadequate. Since he has the actions of alter in his repertoire, these are tied in response to appropriate cues, and if successful, will tend to replace the previous responses in the habit hierarchy. In this case, however, there is no necessary recognition that these responses were originally learned through previous interaction. For example, in our hypothetical case the mother may realize that her manner of handling the child's disobedience is ineffectual, but in seeking new solutions she may not be aware that she is, in effect, using her husband's responses in thinking about how to deal with her child.

To sum up, through these ways of learning the role demands of society are made part of the person and become "internalized." As many have observed, and as Wrong has said, "The normative structure of society is more than an environmental obstacle which the actor must take into account in pursuit of his goals in the same way as he takes into account physical laws; it becomes internal, psychological, and self-imposed, as well. Parsons developed this view that social norms are constitutive rather than merely regulative of human nature before he was influenced by psychoanalytic theory, but Freud's theory of the super-ego has become the source and model for the conception. . . ." (31)

It is valuable, also, to take a developmental view. Goodman (14) has outlined the process of acquisition of components of self-other systems through socialization. Social interaction, however primitive, precedes language, and interaction in this preverbal situation takes place through a "conversation of gestures." Differential reactions on the part of significant others, mainly parents and siblings, tell the child whether his behavior is appropriate or not and lay the basis for self-evaluation. With the increasing ability of the child to use language, the socialization process proceeds with greater rapidity and in greater depth. As the child learns to use language, the range of behavior that he can symbolize increases at a phenomenal rate. At first this symbolic interchange between himself and others is limited to discrete actions of specific persons. At a later time he begins to deal with larger segments of behavior and even whole roles (the period Mead refers to as "play"). The role-taking can be suddenly overt, as with the child who actively and dramatically plays the role of the parent. In this way the child builds up a repertoire of roles which permits him to interact in a variety of situations. Our culture encourages children to play roles that are most likely to be required of them as adults, meanwhile discouraging certain others which may be disruptive to current or future development. Through such role-playing, children learn what to do and what not to do, what role elements are of the can-and-should variety, and what elements are proscribed, falling into the realm of behavior to be avoided. The role-playing is carried out under conditions of play or practice, with little or no censure, so that the first faltering learning trials take place in a nonpunitive environment.

Early role-playing is a transient, unorganized process. Expectations for performance in various roles differ, of course, and the separate learning situations are not systematically related. The understanding is, one might say, of a series of dyads, rather than of a society. It is when the child, growing older, finds himself in more complicated situations in which he must respond to the expectations of several people at the same time, must balance these demands, must assign them priority and integrate them, that the further development of personality takes place. The family, clearly, is the social situation which requires these kinds of behavior, as the child is put into contact successively with the family members. The analysis by Parsons (26) of the demands upon the child for differentiation of types of interpersonal relationships as he matures in the nuclear family illustrates this clearly. Here one will recognize also the importance of Mead's noting participation in organized games as a learning context for such complex demands. The expectations for the child's behavior now derive not only from specific persons but also from complex social systems.

"I-Them," "They-Me," and "I-Me" Relationships

The relationships between a person and other people are the raw material for that part of the personality with which we are concerned. Analytically, personality is a set of learned self-other relationships or systems, themselves constituted of thousands and thousands of remembered expectations, appraisals of one's own performance by self and others, the resultant perceived conformity or deviance (or success or failure) of the action, and the consequent rewards or disapprovals given by society. A basic classification of the resulting self-other systems is expressed by the grammatical construction which describes the relationship. In any thoughts or statements descriptive of one's relations with others either the person is the subject, and the other the object—or the reverse is true. Thus, there are subject and object aspects of any specific component of the self-other system, centering, of course, on some social episodes involving expectations, performance, and appraisals, and including the person and a significant other or others.

This gives rise, therefore, to two major kinds of relations. The first is the "they-me" relationship, in which the person is the object of another's actions, expectations, or attitudes, such as "He doesn't want me to do that," "She approves of what I have just done," "My brother always got along well with me." The second is the "I-them" type, where the object is some other person. Here we find statements or observations of this kind: "I do not think they are fair," "I demand that he do that," "I will be angry if he fails to live up to his promise," and so on.

Two other possible relationships come to mind. One of these is the "they-them" type, where others are both the subject and the object. This is not constitutive of the self-other system, since it involves interaction in which the person is neither subject nor object.

It is the other logical possibility, where the person himself is both the subject and the object, that captures the imagination. What of the general class of relationships of the "I-me" type? Examples are: "I am content with myself," "I expect that I will be able to do this," "I should not demand so much of myself." Perhaps at first glance this does not appear to be part of the self-other system as described above. In fact, it has been recognized as a most fundamental part.

How does the "I-me" component of the self-other system develop? The individual, when looking or acting toward himself as an object, must initially do so from the point of view of some significant other person. For several reasons, this viewpoint becomes dissociated from any specific person, and the "I-me" component of the self thus is generated over time from a number of "they-me" relationships.

How would the situation develop in which the person is no longer able to recall or identify the other in the interpersonal relation, that is, the other who was involved? It appears that both generalization and the inability to discriminate are sources of the "I-me" type of relationship. The "I-me" relationship is the product of a body of learning generalized from interaction with a number of reference figures now nameless because their identity has been lost in countless learning trials. In the most frequent case the information derived about one's self from interaction with others has been given by a great many people so that no specific individual remains linked to this self-other relationship. This is true about basic components of the self such as size, sex, ability, or appearance, and also one's conformity to and deviance from norms widely shared in society. This is one source, then, of the "generalized other" as described by Mead: that which is generalized is no longer identified with any specific other.

Secondly, there is a companion process also leading to generalization, namely, a lack of ability to discriminate on the part of the child in his early interactions with his parents. In these interactions a child's experience has been so limited that he has no basis for differentiating (discriminating) between the reactions of his parents and their demands upon him and the reactions and demands of the entire objective world. In largest part this inability to discriminate exists because communication between parent and infant is preverbal, and the infant lacks symbolic tools to facilitate discrimination between different sources of reward and punishment. What is learned from parents thus is viewed as inherent in the world at large, that is, in the generalized social order. It follows that elements of personality thus acquired provide a good foundation upon which the further process of generalization mentioned above may proceed. For these two reasons, then, the child develops a major component of his personality consisting of self-other relationships of the "I-me" type.

The question of identity, or what might be called the "core-periphery" issue, can now be analyzed. Every person experiences some part of his personality that he feels is more truly his than are other parts. How is one to explain this universal feeling? It seems that there are components of the personality—certain groupings of self-other relationships—that are highly determining of the individual's behavior. In view of the foregoing discussion it appears that these would be primarily of the "I-me" type, in which the perception of one's self in relation to others has been laid down early and frequently, both from powerful figures such as parents and also from a broad and diverse group of human beings, so that these come to constitute his sense of identity. The interchanges and expectations with other specific persons may be of less significance. One is willing to put on a front for them; but their demands are viewed as superficial, and, when in conflict with the "true self," conformity to these relationships—primarily of the "I-them" or "they-me" type—is set aside and the "I-me" set of expectations dominates.

It is not suggested, and it does not follow, that the "I-me" components of personality bear any necessary relationship to components of personality that are repressed and constitute the unconscious aspects of the self-other systems. The fact is that, in the course of interaction with other persons controlling rewards and punishments, experiences occur in which the individual is punished for failure to live up to the expectations of others about his performance—or to his own expectations for his performance where these have been dissociated from the original reference figures (as in the "I-me" relationship in which the individual punishes himself). In these cases the anticipation of failure and punishment may lead to the repression of thoughts of this specific relationship and its concomitants. In this sense, this specific self-other unit of the personality is lost from the conscious repertoire; it is not part of the self-reportable area of personality.

Of course, the components of the personality which are repressed and the components which constitute the "I-me" type *may* overlap; the degree of overlap would vary from one individual to the next. But there should be no confusion between these two distinct aspects of personality. Whether or not the early and generalized learning of the kind leading to "I-me" systems becomes repressed depends on the characteristics of the interaction process, that is, the type of situation in which the generalized material was learned. To repeat, the "I-me" and the repressed components of personality are not necessarily correlated.

Motivation and Role Behavior

What are the implications of the point of view advanced above for motivation and behavior? The answer is simple and straightforward. The individual, because of his previously acquired desire to conform to others' expectations, is motivated to live up to these standards, and his sense of well-being or satisfaction depends on such conformity. The self-other relationship leads to an individual's appraisal of himself as being good or bad, according to the degree to which he lives up to another's expectation. The importance of the self-appraisal to the individual varies according to the significance of the other person's evaluation of him, which, in turn, is based, in the last analysis, on the degree to which the other controls (or once controlled) rewards and punishments. The consequence of self-appraisal and of perceived adequacy or inadequacy is to increase or decrease an individual's self-esteem or self-respect.

It is evident that we are not talking about all motivation, or even all social motivation. However, a significant part of motivated activity in social situations is triggered by the individual's perception of present discrepancies between expectations and his own level of performance or, secondly, his perception of anticipated discrepancies. Where these are anticipated the individual believes that he will be unable to conform to others' standards for him, and the result is fear of or anxiety over possible failure.

Specific kinds of behavior, and motives inferred therefrom, such as a desire for dominance, achievement, or affiliation, frequently will depend on the demands for such behavior by others and the specific self-other relationships which are generating the concern of the individual about his performance. Thus, where achievement is concerned, the expression of behavior from which an "achievement motive" can be named may depend on the existence of a set of reference figures whose expectations for performance in a given context, for example, in school, are to reach a high level of success relative to others.

It must be understood that this powerful source of individual motivation does not come only from the pressures of the immediate or local social system. The general concept identifying those persons to whom an individual refers his behavior to check on its appropriateness and its value is the reference set.* The fundamental question

---

* This concept, developed by Kemper (17), incorporates the earlier idea of the reference group as set forth by Sherif (28) and by Kelley (16) with the concept of role set as advanced by Merton (22). It refers to that multiple set of figures (persons or groups) to whom, in whatever role, the individual refers his behavior.

in understanding motivation is the degree to which the members of an individual's reference set are those whose presence is immediate and proximate, and with whom he is engaged in day-to-day interaction, as contrasted with more distant figures. Indeed, we might refer to this as the proximal-distal characteristic of self-other systems. The assumption that the individual seeks social approval and that persons move in the direction of resolving the demands upon them by conformity to the greatest pressures does not refer solely to the impact of the local social system. The analysis of local expectancies is but the first step, the first appraisal of demands with which one is concerned in his analysis of behavior. He is next concerned with the impact of reference figures who are not present in the immediate social system, with those persons from an earlier part of life, from another year or another place, with the different drummers some men march to, with the influence of dead poets and distant heroes.*

Many men have as members of their reference set persons other than their immediate family or peer group—individuals or groups who are not presently living, such as fictional or religious figures who are far beyond the local social system. Any individual's gallery of reference figures is populated by representatives from a vast range of possibilities—earlier friends, great figures in history, spirits, men yet to be born.

Moreover, most of the significant others who generate motivation are those whose actual relationship to the self has been forgotten or generalized into "I-me" relationships. The major body of motivation coming from "I-me" relationships can be described as a maintenance of self-esteem; it is the pursuit of an adequate or superior performance of some expected task for which the significant appraiser of the outcome has become one's own self. The early, generalized learning described previously leaves the person deeply dependent on self-appraisal for his sense of satisfaction; being true to his core identity is fundamental to his self-esteem.

Thus we see that the vast range of significant others and their demands free the individual from purely immediate pressures of the local social system and provide a much broader basis for his actions.

* See Robert N. Wilson's study of poets' reference sets (30).

SOCIALIZATION IN LATER LIFE

Need for Socialization after Childhood

The socialization that an individual receives in childhood cannot be fully adequate as preparation for the tasks demanded of him in later years. As individuals mature, they move through a sequence of statuses corresponding to different stages in the life cycle (12). Even though some of the expectations of society are relatively stable through the life cycle, many others change from one age to the next. We know that society demands that the individual meet these changed expectations, and demands that he alter his personality and behavior to make room in his life for newly significant persons such as his family members, his teachers, his employers, and his colleagues at work.

The effectiveness of childhood socialization certainly is greater in relatively unchanging societies. Cultural prescriptions of a powerful nature define the usual sequence of statuses and roles that individuals are to assume during their life span. The process of development and differentiation goes along in step with physical maturation— increases in stature, strength, capacity—that permits the individual to meet the enlarged demands upon him associated with new statuses. The increased demands are timed according to age or growth and may be thought of as developmental tasks. Further advances of the individual to greater differentiation of his relationships with others occur according to certain schedules which integrate his capabilities with age-graded requirements of the society. For example, enrollment in school may occur at the age when the child's physical, linguistic, and social skills enable him to deal with the formal educational system.

Also, in such quiet societies, stability comes from the continuity over time of the significant others with whom one is involved. The earliest groups of significant persons remain on the scene through much of one's life. Parents may live on through one's middle years; friendships may persist through much of the life span; one marries into a homogamous group whose expectations are similar to those of prior reference figures. All of this enables socialization to be developmental in nature, that is, to occur in a regular progression from infancy through old age, and for anticipatory socialization for later-life roles to be more effective.

However, even in such relatively unchanging societies one cannot be socialized in childhood to handle successfully all of the roles he will confront in the future. Socialization in later years builds on attitudes and skills acquired earlier, using them as a foundation for later, more demanding learning. It is also true that for reasons fundamental to social organization individuals at certain age periods cannot be socialized completely for roles they may occupy in the future; socialization into the marital role is a case in point. There will be, also, some cultural discontinuities, as Benedict has pointed out (5), so that successive roles to be learned do not build upon each other and even may conflict with what was learned earlier.

The situation for most men is much more difficult, because they live in complex and changing societies. The inadequacies of early socialization for the role the person will play during his lifetime are much greater. The geographical mobility associated with the modern age and the social mobility characteristic of the achievement-oriented open-class society both contribute to the characteristically unforeseeable career pattern of modern man. The heterogeneity of subcultures in complex modern societies compounds the effects of mobility by the novel and unpredictable role demands placed on the individual. So, also, do the rapid social changes occurring during a lifetime render inadequate much childhood learning: technological obsolescence in one's occupation, shifts in sexual folkways, opportunities for equality in employment for minority group members, are but a few of a myriad of examples that might be set forth. Discontinuities between what is expected in successive roles are greater; the inabilities of the socializing agents to do an effective job rise as the rate of change increases; subgroups with deviant values emerge which do not prepare the child for performance of the roles expected of him by the larger society. Agents may be missing, as in broken homes, or key institutions or agencies lacking, as in the absence of an educational system in counties in Virginia when the public schools were closed; the parent himself may be inadequate to the task because he no longer cares or understands.

Faced with these challenges, complex and changing societies might try to lay the groundwork for the necessary learning in later life, when the child will be confronted with adult roles as yet only dimly seen, by providing the individual with initiative, creativity, the power of self-determination, insight, flexibility, and intelligent response to new conditions; to move, that is, away from indoctrination and habit formation toward development of broadly useful traits and skills enabling him to meet a variety of social demands. This, of course, is a familiar educational theory, deriving from changes introduced by John Dewey and others in the past fifty years. From the sociological viewpoint these changes are seen as an attempt by American society to provide for effective socialization of its members through life without being dependent on societal stability.

This is desirable but not sufficient; modern societies must provide for resocialization into roles for which the person has not been developmentally prepared. Societal institutions evolve that are specifically devoted to resocialization of the child or adult, much as the school and family are devoted to developmental socialization. Newly visible deficiencies in training are met by new resocialization efforts, good illustrations being the marital and parental roles. Poor developmental socialization is caused by inattention on the part of the child's parents, the absence of many siblings in the home, general decreased responsibility of children for helping parents in their duties, and so on. As a consequence, programs and institutions are emerging which are devoted to parent and family life education.

Limits of Later-Life Socialization

Given the need for adult socialization, what are the potentialities for new learning, and for change in personality, of the individual after his formative childhood years? The limits of socialization in later life are set by the biological capacities of an individual and by the effects of earlier learning or the lack of it. The effectiveness of later-life socialization is a consequence of the interaction of these two restrictions with the level of technology achieved by the society in its socialization methods. The latter depend primarily on the knowledge available about human behavior and to a lesser extent on mechanical developments; the remarks that follow assume a given level of socialization technology.

A substantial portion of the human raw material of society that is biologically inadequate in one respect or another is removed from natural progression through the life cycle by one of several methods and hence does not appear in the usual later-life socialization situations. By and large, the demands of a society upon adults are tailored to the capacities of the average man, and socialization proceeds without interference from biological limitations.

There are, nevertheless, two ways in which biological restrictions lead to limitations on later-life socialization. The first of these occurs primarily in an open-class society with a high level of achievement motivation. Here upward mobility into ever more demanding roles may lead an individual to positions in which he is unable to meet the challenges because of limited intelligence, strength, or other biological attributes. The second occurs when war or another disaster destroys the protection given to individuals by society from the direct impact of nature, and persons biologically adequate for the roles they will meet in the course of their normal civilized life cycle may suddenly find themselves unable to live under new and primitive conditions.

The effects of earlier learning, or the lack of them, are the other limits on later-life socialization. First we must recognize the durable qualities of early childhood learning. Socialization occurring during childhood correctly receives primary emphasis in research and theory. The potency and durability of the learning that occurs during this period are assumed on the basis of the frequency of learning situations, their primacy in the career of the organism, and the intensity of the rewards and punishments administered. Moreover, what is learned in childhood is difficult to change because much of it was learned under conditions of partial reinforcement.

In addition, it is held by many (and believed to be of utmost importance) that during early socialization the bulk of the unconscious material of the personality is accumulated, and the inertia established in the individual personality by its unconscious components, relatively inaccessible as they are to change through simple socialization procedures, is the cause of its manifest continuity. One might add that probably the characteristic modes of defense also are established early, thus painting the basic colors of personality for the life span.

Granted that there are enduring qualities to childhood learning, the effects of such learning on later-life socialization are more complicated than they may seem to be on quick consideration. It is not only that early learning interferes with and limits later learning. This is just one of several effects. Rather, it is the relationship of earlier learning, or its absence, to later learning which determines whether it will limit or facilitate adult socialization.

In some cases there is discontinuity and conflict between earlier and later learning. Later-life socialization requires replacement of the earlier with the later, of the old with the new, rather than building upon the existing personality base; the contrast in the premarital and postmarital roles of the American middle-class female is an outstanding example of this discontinuity.

In other instances, the childhood learning may facilitate later learning, if the elements learned first are compatible with what is to be learned in later life. As is pointed out later, adult socialization frequently consists of creating new combinations of old response elements; if these elements have been well learned, they may facilitate learning the adult role.

Sometimes it is the absence of certain childhood learning that affects later-life socialization. Here, at first glance, we would think that the absence of childhood learning would provide a clean slate for the later-life socialization effort, and that the absence of possibly competing responses would make the adult's learning tasks much easier. Training the new bride how to cook, or teaching a manual trade to the previously untutored adolescent, seems easier than changing skills that may already exist. This is true in many cases, but we should be cautious. It is doubtful that one comes on a role in later life without any fragments at all of relevant socialization; the inexperienced mother may seem to know little, but she knows something, and, even more, she has response elements for the role performance that are not manifest at the conscious level.

The absence of early learning clearly will hinder later-life socialization when something that should have been acquired as a basis for learning in later years in fact was not. It has been suggested (10) that the occurrence of critical periods in the life cycle, now demonstrated in subhuman species, may also characterize human development. If there are certain things that must be learned by human beings at specific stages in their development, then failure to learn this material at the appropriate period makes subsequent learning impossible. Such early deficiencies may even affect the learning ability itself. Although we know little as yet about possible critical periods in learning, we can speculate about adulthood; for example, learning certain attitudes during the formative middle years may lay the necessary basis for satisfactory socialization into the old-age role.

What data do we have on the effects of early-life experience? The main evidence comes from case histories obtained in clinical practice (8), and it has a *post hoc* and speculative quality. Recently more attention has been given to empirical studies of continuity in personality and to the durability of early childhood learning. LeVine (19) cites many of these studies with reference to the acquisition of language and enduring political attitudes. Neugarten, in her review (24) of research on the continuity of personality through time, reports that the studies present inconsistent conclusions which vary from study to study and from sample to sample. She states that while the evidence shows "continuity of personality" the larger proportion of the variance in personality at later times remains unaccounted for; that is, it is not predictable from earlier measurements of personality. She concludes that "the nature of personality changes in adulthood may be relatively obscure; but the conviction is a reasonable one that changes do occur." (p. 55)

Many of the existing studies are unsatisfactory in another way. They report on specific personality traits, such as an attitude or some type of response, and the data often are the unintended output of a concern with some other topic. In comparison to the amount of information available about personality development in earlier age periods, we have little knowledge about older age groups. Sewell (27) points out that there are relatively few sharply defined or clearly focused studies of adult socialization concerned with the process by which society, through its subgroups, socializes a person in later life into a specific role or set of roles, with attention given to the changes which may result in measurable personality characteristics. The few prototypical studies which can be cited are primarily in the area of job training or, more broadly, occupational socialization, especially the work of Becker and his colleagues (1).

A study outside of the occupational role that is of special interest is Vincent's work on marital socialization (29). His study demonstrates change in scores on scales of the California Personality Inventory (such as dominance and self-acceptance) as a consequence of marriage. A control group of unmarried persons shows almost no change compared to the married group. Vincent also reports that the amount of change depends in part on the age of the couple at marriage, with those who marry early showing the greatest subsequent change. Other work on adults which may prove valuable comes from family life education. Most of the studies of family life education are highly valuable analyses of how one carries on adult socialization; the observations made in these studies about methods and the causes of change in adult personality are applicable to other adult socialization processes (8).

To summarize, both biological and early-learning limitations on later-life socialization exist, but their exact nature is not understood. Discussion of the problem, and the arguments pro and con, would be clarified by specifying the levels or types of behavior or personality characteristics which one has in mind, for example, political attitudes, feelings about one's father, reactions to authority, or beliefs about God. Much remains to be done, and too little attention has been given to the study of the possibly sizable changes which occur after childhood as a result of deliberate socialization processes by society. The powerful arguments for the potent effects of early-life experiences should not deter the study of large and important changes that may take place in later life.

CHANGES IN CONTENT OF SOCIALIZATION

The substantive content of socialization differs, of course, in important ways at different stages of the life cycle and in different major social institutions. People learn different things at different times and places in their lives.

It is uncertain, however, whether the types as opposed to the substance of the content differ throughout the life cycle. Still the needs for socialization and the effects of learning and biological characteristics in any given case would seem to dictate the nature of the socialization process; and since these vary by life-cycle stages, with the needs and limits of adult socialization being different from those of childhood, it is probable that the types of content vary accordingly. Six such probable changes in content will be discussed.

The most important change, perhaps, is the shift in content from a concern with values and motives to a concern with overt behavior.* Some other changes are described in other aspects of socialization content. These are as follows: from acquisition of new material to a synthesis of the old; from a concern with idealism to a concern with realism; from teaching expectations to teaching how to mediate conflict among expectations; from a concern with general demands of society to a concern with role-specific expectations; and finally, a change from "I-me" components of personality to other components.

Values and Motives versus Overt Behavior

There are three things a person requires before he is able to perform satisfactorily in a role. He must know what is expected of him (both in behavior and in values), must be able to meet the role requirements, and must desire to practice the behavior and pursue the appropriate ends. It can be said that the purposes of socialization are to give a person knowledge, ability, and motivation.

A simple cross-classification of these three concepts with values and behavior establishes a paradigm which helps to analyze changes in the content of socialization through the life cycle. In this paradigm six cells are indicated by letters for simplicity of reference:

	Behavior	Values
Knowledge	A	B
Ability	C	D
Motivation	E	F

Cells A and B indicate respectively that the individual knows what behavior is expected of him and what ends he should pursue; E and F indicate that the individual is motivated to behave in the appropriate ways and to pursue the designated values; C and D

* An analysis of adult socialization in terms of the relative emphasis on these two role components was introduced to the Social Science Research Council Conference by Irving Rosow in his paper, "Forms and Functions of Adult Socialization." See also Merton (23).

indicate that the individual is able to carry out the behavior and to hold appropriate values.*

With respect to changes during the life cycle, the emphasis in socialization moves from motivation to ability and knowledge, and from a concern with values to a concern with behavior.

The highest priority in childhood socialization is represented by Cell F, namely, to take the basic drives of the infant and transform them over time into desires for recognition and approval and finally to the pursuit of more specific cultural values. Early-life socialization thus emphasizes the control of primary drives, while socialization in later stages deals with secondary or learned motives generated by the expectations of significant others. Except in rare and extreme conditions, adult socialization does not need to teach the individual to control and regulate the gratification of primary drive systems.†

The usual concern of adult socialization is represented by Cell A. Society assumes that the adult knows the values to be pursued in different roles, that he wants to pursue them with the socially appropriate means, and that all that may remain to be done is to teach him what to do. This is illustrated by the case of a military recruit. The training program starts at about the level of "This is a gun" and "This is how it is fired." If there are some things the individual is unable to do (Cell C), the training program seeks to upgrade his ability—for example, by instruction designed to reduce illiteracy. If he is unwilling to carry out his various tasks (Cell D), then motivational training occurs through administration of special rewards and punishments. If it appears that education about values is needed (Cell B), the individual is enrolled in a general orientation course on American values and the purpose of the wars; the "why we fight" training programs are instituted to provide an understanding of the

* The question of being able or unable to hold values may at first seem somewhat peculiar, but the inability involved here arises from conflict within the personality. This instance of inability as a source of deviance in role performance is discussed in greater detail later on.
† The development of secondary motives oriented toward social approval (in a broad sense) and based on learning associated with the satisfaction of primary motives is a part of socialization but is not commensurate with it. It is true that sometimes one speaks of a person being unsocialized because of what appears to be a greater concern with the gratification of primary than of secondary motivation. But one also correctly calls unsocialized a person with deviant values and bizarre behavior, even when the primary drive system itself has been well socialized.

appropriate ends to be sought. If the individual has serious conflicts within himself but does his best, therapeutic procedures are instituted to solve this problem, which lies in Cell D. Only in the last analysis, when other possible types of deficiencies in socialization have been ruled out, is it assumed that there is a problem in motivation toward the appropriate values, the case represented by Cell F. Such men are critical of the value system of their society; in our country they may be pacifists, Communists, or members of other groups which reject traditional American values. Sometimes resocialization efforts are launched in such cases, but more often retraining of these individuals is considered to be an impossible task, and they are jailed, ignored, or relegated to marginal, inconsequential positions.

In general, then, socialization after childhood deals primarily with overt behavior in the role and makes little attempt to influence motivation of a fundamental kind or to influence basic values. Society is willing to spend much less time in redirecting the motivation and values of adults than of children; for the latter it is understood that this is a necessary task of the institutions involved, such as the family, and they are organized to carry out this function.

Why should this difference exist? Probably it stems directly from the limitations on learning in later life, which makes impractical any attempt at thorough resocialization. Irving Rosow has asked if adult socialization can, in fact, generate suitable beliefs and attitudes, suitable motivation for certain types of performance, or whether the limitations on learning are such that the socializing agent must deal with overt performance only. It may be that the costs are too high and that it simply is not efficient from society's point of view to spend too much time on teaching an old dog new tricks. Perhaps an intensive and costly resocialization effort can be made for adults only when the need for a certain kind of manpower is unusually great and the question of efficiency becomes secondary to the demand for personnel.

Society has at least two major solutions to this possible problem. One is anticipatory: selection is made of candidates for an adult organization to screen out those who do not have appropriate motives and values for the anticipated roles. This procedure helps to assure that those who enter the organization will not present difficult problems for the socialization program. In this way adults probably get sorted out, more or less, and placed in social situations where they fit best in terms of the values and motives learned in their early-life socialization.

A second solution, which Rosow has pointed out, is that society may accept as evidence of satisfactory socialization conforming behavior alone, foregoing any concern with value systems. This entails risk, as he indicates, for if the social system undergoes stress, the conformity, since it is superficial, may break down rapidly.

As a last resort, the remaining instances of deviance in need of resocialization—the genuinely tough cases where the appropriate values have not been internalized—can be processed through the special correctional institutions (prisons, hospitals, etc.) of the society at large.

Acquisition of New Material versus Synthesis of Old Material

As a person moves through the life cycle he accumulates an extensive repertoire of responses, both affective and behavioral. These are organized according to roles and, at a more specific level, by episodes within a role. These responses can be detached from the contexts in which they have been learned and used, and joined with others in new combinations suitable as social behavior responsive to the complex demands of adulthood. We can say, therefore, that the content acquired in adult socialization is not so much new material as it is the aggregation and synthesis of elements from a storehouse of already-learned responses, with perhaps the addition of several fragments that are newly learned when necessary to fill out the required social acts. The usual objective of socialization in the later-life stages is to get one to practice a new combination of skills already acquired, to combine existing elements into new forms, to trim and polish existing material, rather than to learn wholly new complexes or responses, as in the case of the relatively untrained child, for whom the socialization effort starts with little more than initial intelligence and primary drives.

Idealism and Realism

The third change in content is the transformation of idealism into realism. As the individual matures, society demands that he become more realistic and lay aside his childish idealism. Early learning encompasses the formal status structure; later learning takes into account the actual and/or informal status structure. One designates as cynical a person who doubts that the actual and the formal are the same. However, we think of a person as naive if he does not make this distinction. In socialization the child is shielded from contact with the informal systems of society—or, at least, knowledge of these is not formally taught. This serves to maintain and legitimize the formal status differentiations and to protect them from change. But at later stages in the life cycle, for the system to work effectively, the realistic aspects of status differentiation also must be taught.

Closely related is learning to distinguish between ideal role prescriptions and what is actually expected of one in a role. Here, as in the foregoing, the inculcation of ideal role prescriptions results in a desirable idealism which strengthens and perpetuates the ideal of the society. As the child matures he is taught to realize that there is a distinction between the ideal and the real, and learns to take his part in society according to the realistic expectations of others, rather than attempting conformity to ideal norms.

Resolving Conflicts; Meta-prescriptions

The fourth type of change is to a greater concern with teaching the individual to mediate conflicting demands. As one moves through the life cycle, he is forced to develop methods of selecting among conflicting role prescriptions. The possible conflicts between the prescriptions of reference set members are classifiable into two basic types. First, there is intrarole conflict of two kinds: (a) the prescriptions of two or more individuals for the same aspect of a role may conflict: thus, the wife and the employer may differ in their prescriptions for the individual's job performance; (b) prescriptions of just one individual about different aspects of the role may be in conflict; the wife may expect her husband to be both companion with and taskmaster to his son.

Second, there is interrole conflict, again classifiable into two subtypes: (a) conflict between two or more individuals about two separate roles; for example, the employer's demands for job performance conflict with the wife's demands for familial performance; (b) conflict between the expectations of one individual for performance in two different roles, as in the case where the wife has conflicting expectations for her husband's behavior at home and on the job.

The need to learn how to handle such conflicts occurs to a greater extent in later life for at least two reasons. First, children tend to be shielded by society from the realities of life; and if the cultural norm is that children should be protected from seeing life's conflicts, then it follows that nothing will be taught about ways of mediating them. Second, in later life there are more roles and more complexity within roles, so that a much greater possibility exists of role conflict. To put it differently, the reference set of adults is considerably larger than that of children; their social systems are more extensive and more numerous. They have a past, for one thing; and they have occupational roles, as well as additional family roles gained through marriage. They are attuned more often to distant reference figures than they were as children, when their reference sets included mainly those near them.

Thus, as a person ages, he learns the ways of conflict resolution which Ralph Linton (20) has described so well: avoiding the situation, withdrawing acceptably from conflict, and scheduling conflicting demands in temporal sequence, so that the conflict disappears. Also, as Howard Becker has pointed out, he learns another major method of conflict resolution, that is, to compromise between the opposing demands.

There is another important method of conflict resolution which may have been overlooked or at least has not been given formal conceptualization. In every society there are well-recognized prescriptions for solving certain kinds of conflicts that arise from the competing demands of reference set members. These prescriptions for mediating role conflict can be called *meta-prescriptions*. Such meta-prescriptions govern the resolution of conflict between demands on one's time and loyalties, and usually, although not always, pertain to interrole rather than intrarole conflict.* Examples of meta-

---

* A current study of executive personality and achievement carried out by the author and his colleagues and mentioned in the Preface has collected substantial data on the meta-prescriptions for resolving role conflict between the demands of parents and children, one's boss and his work colleagues, wife and employer, and so on. These meta-prescriptions may differ from one person to the next, and result in relatively more or fewer conflict resolutions being made in, say, the direction of favoring the prescriptions of one's work environment as contrasted

prescriptions are "Do what your employer asks of you, even if it means that you have little time for your children," and "Side with your wife when she disciplines the children, even if you think she is wrong." Meta-prescriptions, therefore, guide the process of compromise and dictate whether the solutions should be one-sided, as in the two examples given above, or more on a half-and-half basis, such as "Save at least three nights a week for your family, even if there is work you should be doing." It seems that a noticeable change in the content of socialization in later-life periods is the attention given to ways of resolving conflict through such meta-prescriptions.

Increase in Specificity

The fifth characteristic of change in socialization content is along the dimension of generality-specificity; that is, whether what is taught applies to many social situations or to just a few. This dimension can be applied to both components, values and means, of role prescriptions. There is no reason to maintain that values necessarily are general, and that methods of achieving them are specific. This is noted only because of the tendency to define values as something general; the concept is not being used in this sense.

A child is trained both deliberately and unwittingly by socializing agents in the goals and behavior appropriate for his sex. There are male and female styles of doing many different things, and these are learned early. These characteristics are general, in the sense that they are required in a variety of situations he will confront in society, either as major components or as necessary coloring to other aspects of his behavior.

The case is similar for cultural differences in basic values, such as those related to achievement, to nature, to the family, and indeed for all those general value orientations, to use Florence Kluckhohn's phrase (18), which help to distinguish major cultural groups. They are acquired early (and, in contrast to sex roles, with perhaps less deliberate instruction), and they give shape and tone to the performance of many roles in society.

It also is true that a person is socialized for his socioeconomic posi-

with his home. These appear to be fairly powerful predictors of differential achievement.

tion, a process that Charles E. Bidwell speaks of as socialization into a status level or a style of life.[*] Again, general skills and values are learned, appropriate to carrying out in a certain manner a number of specific role demands for behavior. The values and behavior appropriate to a social class position, to a prestige level in life, usually are acquired in childhood; and, as was true with respect to sex roles and basic cultural values, some part of what is learned is gained outside of any deliberate formal training program.

One would have to say that these general values of one's culture are, on the whole, acquired in childhood. True, as Bidwell points out, there is some socialization into value systems of a given social class during the college age. He notes that one function of fraternities in certain colleges is to carry on this kind of socialization into a social class level higher than that of the individual's family or origin. The existence of formal socializing agencies with this recognized function is understood as a response to the "legitimate" need for resocialization resulting from the upward social mobility in American life in which the individual moves from one subculture to another, with corresponding differences in expectations.

Doubtless there are other occasions in which the general values are the content of socialization at later age periods, but these are not easy to identify. In most instances the content of later-life socialization tends to be role-specific, rather than general in nature.

Fewer "I-Me" Relationships

This final life-cycle comparison arises from the basic view presented earlier that part of personality consists of self-other systems. From what has been said, it follows that the content acquired in later stages of the life cycle would involve fewer of the "I-me" type of self-other relationships and more of the objective "they-me" and "I-them" components. Reviewing the reasons for the development of this kind of self-other system, one realizes that the causes for the lack of identification of the significant person or persons, and the resultant use of "I" in their place, exist to a much lesser degree in adulthood. At later ages the source of the material which is acquired

[*] Charles E. Bidwell, "Some Aspects of Pre-adult Socialization," paper prepared for the Social Science Research Council Conference.

is more readily identifiable; the "they" involved usually is quite clear. Moreover, with the growth of power in maturity, one increases the degree to which he is the instigator of the action and consequently is engaged more frequently in, and thus thinks about himself as, the "I-them" relationship.

If one equates the "I-me" component of personality with the core personality, with "identity," as indicated in the discussion earlier, then he could say that identity tends to be laid down in largest part in early stages of the life cycle. This is true to a degree, of course, but as was said in considering the limiting effects of childhood experiences, it is overemphasized. Not uncommonly, dramatic shifts in identity do occur at later stages of the life cycle, since significant persons may have an unusual impact on a person's appraisal of his own basic characteristics.

RELATIONSHIP TO THE SOCIALIZING AGENT

The relationship between the individual and the socializing agent or agency may change through the life cycle. Is the relationship between parent and child paralleled by that between teacher and student, minister and church member, husband and wife, employer and employee? What can one say as to whether the characteristics of a successful socialization relationship between two individuals differ according to the age of the person being socialized?

There is no single commonly accepted way of analyzing the relationships among persons. Among those which have had a wide use are the earlier "Chicago school" description of intergroup processes by such terms as "competition" and "cooperation," the "pattern variables" of Talcott Parsons (25), the factor analyses of parent-child relationships (4), the interaction categories used in Bales' small-group analyses (26), and the formalistic analyses of types of dyadic relationships in the tradition of German sociology, to name a few. Other ways of describing the relationships refer to the relative power of individuals or the relative prestige, emulation, or frequency of contact. From these, three characteristics of interpersonal relationships seem of special value in describing the relationships of individuals to socializing agents.

Formality of the Relationship

The first characteristic is the degree of formality or institutionaliza-
tion of the relationship.* One way of assessing formality is to inquire into the nature of the roles regulating the interpersonal relationship. In many instances the individual being socialized has a
well-prescribed role as a learner; one takes a role to learn a role, so
to speak.

> There are certain social relationships whose primary function in so-
> ciety is to train society's members. In the teacher-pupil and the parent-
> child relationships the broad and dominant purpose is the physical care
> and training of the child so that he may become a socially suitable
> member of society. The major function in these relationships is to pro-
> duce, if you will, certain kinds of behavior and attitudes in the person
> being trained. In such relationships the role of the child is formally
> given as that of a person being socialized. (7)

Socialization at later ages quite often does not require the individual to take the role of one being socialized. There are exceptions, as
in an occupational apprenticeship, or situations where prior socialization has been inadequate and the person is required to go through
a resocialization process in a specified role, for example, in a correctional institution. Nevertheless, socialization of husbands into marital roles by their wives (and vice versa), socialization of the adult
by the child into the role of parent, socialization into most types of
work, gradual shifts into the old-age role—these and many others do
not require the person being socialized to take the formally specified
role of a learner.

Yonina Talmon has pointed out that there is another sense in
which a socialization relationship may be formal, depending on
whether the socializing agent or agency constitutes or represents a
formal organization, such as an army unit, a school, or a corporation,
or is, instead, an informal primary group, such as the family or a
friendship group.

These two components of formality yield a fourfold classification:
formal organization, role of learner specified; formal organization,

* This analysis has benefited from Dr. Yonina Talmon's paper, "Comparative
Analysis of Adult Socialization," prepared for the Social Science Research
Council Conference, and also from her comments on a previous draft of this
section.

role of learner not specified; informal organization, role of learner specified; informal organization, role of learner not specified. Where the organization is formal and the role of learner is specified, perhaps the best example from early in the life cycle is the student. Examples from later stages of life are the training of the new military recruit and systematic "on the job" training for an occupation. Talmon has pointed out that even within formal organizations with specified socialization roles much of the socialization still occurs through informal processes, outside of the specified roles. Studies have made clear that the primary group often is the main agency of socialization within these formal institutions. Thus, while training may be acquired in a well-defined role, a great deal of indirect, unplanned training takes place through informal discussion and perhaps unconscious identification with role models.

In the next case, where the organization is formal but the role of learner is not specified, the person has to learn as best he can through observation, gleaning information here and there. In the third type, where the socialization agency is an informal group but the learner's role has been prescribed, the child in his family is the archetype. Finally, the important case where both the agency is informal and no role is specified is exemplified by peer-group socialization, as of the child in his neighborhood, and by adult socialization into a new social class or community status or into a wider family circle through marriage.

The comparison of socialization at various stages suggests differences of many kinds, but the most striking is that much of adult socialization takes place in formal organizations without a clearly specified role for the learner, while the child, in sharp contrast, is socialized by informal groups in which he has a well-defined learner's role. Much adult socialization thus is allowed to proceed through trial-and-error learning; for children, however, the process is regulated by specification of rights and duties and provides opportunities for supervision and guidance to help shape the appropriate responses, and protected occasions for practice without punishment.

Power and Support in the Relationship

Another aspect of the relationship between persons and their socializing agents can be referred to as its quality. An analysis of the pertinent characteristics of relative power and support has been made by Straus.* Many methods of describing the parent-child relationship have been used, and in the past two decades a number of factor analyses,† intended to reduce the various descriptions to their common elements, have shown that power and affectivity are the two major dimensions underlying the various ways of describing relationships. This empirical discovery points to the importance of these two dimensions. The first indicates the degree to which the socializing agent (the parent in these particular studies) exerts dominance or authority in relationship to his child, as against being permissive or democratic or even, in some cases, submissive. The second indicates the degree to which there is a highly affective relationship between the parent and child, in contrast with one of low affectivity or "affective neutrality," to use Parsons' term (25). The affectivity, of course, can range in direction from positive to negative, from love to hate; it is the amount of affectivity that is the issue.

Most studies of adult interaction have analyzed small *ad hoc* group processes such as leadership development and problem solving. Factor analyses of these data on interaction among adults reveal the same characteristics of power and affectivity to be the two basic dimensions (6), and it seems likely that this would also be true in adult socialization relationships such as those between recruits and drill sergeants in a military setting, or in the interaction of a newly married couple.

Use of the dimensions of power and affectivity in a fourfold classification will serve to identify different types of relationships. In this way interpersonal situations can be contrasted. In the case of childhood, a parent who rejects his child and is dominant can be contrasted with one who loves his child and is easy-going and permissive. In adulthood, the conditions under which an occupation is being learned in one instance may involve little affectivity and little difference in power, while other situations may involve considerable exercise of authority of the agent over the trainee, with more feeling being involved.

* Murray A. Straus, "Power and Support Structure of the Family in Relation to Socialization," paper prepared for the Social Science Research Council Conference and now published in *Journal of Marriage and the Family*, Vol. 26, August, 1964.
† Wesley C. Becker recently has reviewed these analyses (4).

The major contrast is between child and adult socialization relationships. It is clear that the child is socialized in a context of high affectivity and high power, and the adult in a sharply contrasting situation of affective neutrality and little power differentiation. Straus points out in his paper that the "high power," "high support" (or positive affect) relationship leads to the acquisition by children of deep-seated motives and values. Other investigators theorizing about the child's acquisition of the basic parental and cultural values also take this view: that the environment where the socializing agent is powerful and the affective rewards and punishments are great is the one where the fundamental components of personality are established.

The adult socialization context does not have these characteristics and is not conducive to the inculcation of basic values. Adult socialization probably requires a relationship resembling that of childhood to effect equivalent changes in basic values through socialization. This relationship may occur in rare and usually noninstitutionalized instances, for example, in adult religious conversion, where the submissive relationship and highly affective interchange with a religious figure underlie the radical shift in the value system. Another example is the relationship in prisoner-of-war camps. Recent research on "brainwashing" and the breakdown of resistance to enemy values shows this context to be one where the captors use their extreme power in deliberate manipulation of the whole range of affect from rejection and hate, on the one hand, to support and overt sympathy, on the other, thus bringing the prisoner into a position similar to that of a child with his parent. Goffman's analysis (13) of the characteristics of settings which are conducive to identity change, such as mental hospitals, bears on this point.

It appears that if society is to undertake basic resocialization of adults in respect to motives and values, it might well institutionalize in some form the high power and affectivity relationship characteristic of childhood learning.

Group Context of the Person Being Socialized

A third, highly important set of dimensions of the relationship with the socializing agent is derived from the basic classification of socialization contexts presented in Stanton Wheeler's essay, which follows. Two questions are raised about the person being socialized:

is he being socialized alone or as a member of a group; and, in either case, is he (or the group) one of a series, passing through the socializing process in succession, or one of a kind? The first distinction, introduced by Becker (3), is between an individual and a collectivity; the second is between serial and disjunctive relationships. These two distinctions, when combined, produce the fourfold classification used by Wheeler.

It is well to ask what variations, if any, exist in these aspects of socialization from one stage of the life cycle to another. A review of the varying contexts leads to the conclusion that there are no regular systematic changes. Consider the situation of the child. The primary socialization of early life occurs in contexts which vary from individual to group, and from serial to disjunctive, relationships. An only child in a family continues in an individual disjunctive relationship, but the eldest child remains in that relationship for only a year or more. Most often, a child is one of a series, passing through the socialization process as an individual. Still, if children are close in age and interaction is encouraged, they may develop a close group relationship and their situation could be described as one of collective disjunctive socialization. Finally, in contrast, in the other major institution of childhood, the school, the children are socialized in what is clearly a collective serial relationship.

Each of these situations has consequences for the socialization process. Older children in families may pass on to the younger learned ways of getting around the parents or, on the other hand, may be active agents of socialization under the monitoring of their parents. Where the children are close in age and act as a group, their solidarity may enable them to influence the course of parental practices. So is it also with children in school, although it is unlikely that children in the early grades ever develop as effective means of influencing procedures as do their seniors in high school or college.

In the later stages of the life cycle we also find the individual in a variety of socialization contexts. In some instances he is alone and in a unique relationship; this characterizes the mutual socialization of spouses in marriage. But in other cases—for example, when a person enters the military system or becomes a member of a church or joins a social club—the relationship is that of a member of a collectivity and is usually of a serial nature.

Apparently there is little systematic change from one type of relationship to another in socialization through the life span. Nevertheless, the distinction between these socialization settings suggests that closer study of their differing effects on the person being socialized may be valuable, whatever age is involved. Brief reflection reminds one that the many studies of family size and birth order in relation to personality characteristics [recently reviewed by Clausen and Williams (11)] are in one sense attempts to measure the effects of being socialized in these four different contexts. Studies of only children, for example, that compare them on achievement with children having siblings can be viewed as studies of the consequences for achievement of socialization in the individual disjunctive relationship, rather than one of the other three types. Research on family size and birth order has not been noted for good theoretical formulation. It may be that this type of conceptual analysis, at a higher level of abstraction, of what the different family structures mean will permit comparisons of family contexts with other socialization contexts of the same theoretical type and so lead to more productive studies than before.

RESOCIALIZATION AS A CONTROL FOR DEVIANT BEHAVIOR

There are always groups in society with different viewpoints on what is regarded as proper; what is deviance from one person's frame of reference may be viewed as conformity by another. Becker, in his recent book, *The Outsiders* (2), has made this point forcefully. Thus, whether or not an individual's behavior or values are deviant always must be determined by reference to the viewpoint of some specific person or group. In the discussion that follows the commonly shared norms of the larger society are used as the frame of reference.

Resocialization is but one among the possible modes of control over deviant behavior which society has at its disposal. It can exclude members from participation; it can isolate them from their fellow human beings; it can utilize severe punishment where the purpose is to influence other possible offenders to change their ways. With all these mechanisms, however, deliberate resocialization by society is probably its most effective mode of control over its deviant members.

In the discussion of the need for later-life socialization, some of

the sources of difficulty the adult may have in meeting the expectations of others were noted: expectations may change; prior socializing agents may be ineffective; the person may be caught in conflicts he cannot solve. Once again we leave out of consideration
here the biological limitations on effective socialization resulting
from low intelligence, sensory disability, and the like, since individuals with such disabling characteristics are gradually removed from
the normal course of development and dealt with in society by insti-
tutionalization.

Types of Deviance

The first task in the analysis of resocialization as a solution to
deviance is to make a conceptual analysis of the types of deviant
behavior. The chart introduced earlier (page 25) presented six types
of content of the socialization effort, namely, knowledge, ability, and
motivation, each in relation to behavior and values. This same chart,
therefore, indicates the six basic types of deviance, corresponding to
failures of the socialization process in the six areas of content.

Consideration of the chart shows that the sources of deviance are
an individual's ignorance, his lack of ability, or his lack of motivation, and that deviance may occur in behavior or values—or both.
The intersection of these three sources with the two possible areas
generates the six basic types of deviance. Illustrations of each
type can be drawn from a familiar family situation involving the
son's academic achievement and the expectations of his parents.

In the first type (Cell A in the chart), the actor is ignorant of the
behavior that is expected of him. Consider the son who knows that
he is required to get good marks but does not yet fully understand
the importance of studying hard and completing homework on time.

In the second type (Cell B), the actor is ignorant of the ends to
be sought. The child may conform behaviorally to his parents' expectations to study hard but does so because he is afraid of their
criticism, not yet understanding that the value he should be pursu-
ing is to obtain outstanding grades.

In the third type (Cell C), the actor deviates in behavior because
of inability to conform. A simple example is a son's inability to
carry out the prescribed studying because of weak eyes or poor
physical condition.

In the fourth type (Cell D), inability is the source of deviance in values. There are familiar instances of how possession of a value may be impossible because of the punishing conflict it produces. Here, the son may not pursue the value of going to college because it involves him in direct competition with his father's record at college, and he cannot tolerate the anxiety this arouses in him. He may still study hard and do well, but does so to avoid criticism by his parents rather than to be admitted to college.

In the last two types (Cells E and F), motivation is the source of deviance. In respect to Cell E, where the deviance is in behavior, the son simply may find studying difficult and unpleasant, being insufficiently motivated to carry out the prescribed action. He may pursue the value of obtaining the grades but seek to achieve them through deviant means such as cheating.

In the final type (Cell F), where the lack of motivation refers to the pursuit of appropriate values, while conformity exists in behavior, there is the familiar case of a person behaving in the right way but for the wrong reason. Thus the son may study hard but reject the parentally prescribed end of continued academic education; he pursues instead the goal of getting a higher rating in the Navy when he graduates from high school.

Note that the types represented in Cells D and F are quite different even though they appear similar. In Cell D, where the person is unable to pursue a given value, it is not because he is unmotivated toward this end, as is true of Cell F. A person can want something he is unable to pursue. Thus the child may wish that he could be interested in college, even though he cannot.

These are the six simple cases of deviance. They are the pure types, which are the building blocks of more complex deviant actions. Two illustrations will show the construction of these complex cases. For example, deviance commonly occurs both in behavior and in values. Where this is true, and the source is ignorance, the obvious illustrations are those of any untutored person: the newborn infant, the hillbilly recruit, the child during his first day at school, the mother of a newborn child. Where the source is lack of motivation, an illustration is the pacifist faced with the expectations of the infantry combat role, in which he neither pursues the end of killing nor wants to engage in combat.

Modes of Control

The modes of attempted control over deviance which are characteristically used by an individual, a group, or a society reflect its theories and assumptions about the causes of deviance and are rooted in its ideas about human nature; for example, whether man is inherently a stupid animal, whether he is possessed by demons or controlled by other supernatural forces, whether he is innately depraved, or burdened with original sin.

In our own society it is deviance in motivation and values (Cell F) which is viewed as most serious. The concept of motivation plays an important role in our theories of why human beings behave as they do, and deviance in motivation is viewed as a serious threat to the social order. If a person does not share with others the values of his society and/or rejects the means used to achieve them, he is untrustworthy and unpredictable as a fellow member of an established social group. It seems that our society is more willing to tolerate deviance stemming from ignorance or lack of ability if only a peron means well, has his heart in the right place, has good intentions.

Because of these beliefs about motivation and the concern with which this type of deviance is viewed, there is a tendency to examine instances of deviance for possible motivational components in order to appraise how serious the deviance is. In return, the deviant person, challenged to account for his behavior and faced with punishments for having the wrong motives—punishments customarily greater than those for deviance from the other two sources—will plead ignorance or lack of ability as the cause for his actions. The result is that considerable time is spent in both legal and informal social control procedures, searching for possible motivational deviance behind the façade of ignorance or lack of ability.

Sometimes it appears that the law, to avoid the difficult problem of appraising the motivational component in deviance, simply assumes that the cause of the deviant act is motivation. Before the law, ignorance or lack of ability rarely constitute a satisfactory excuse for nonconformity. Lack of knowledge that a stop sign has been put on a corner, or a sudden brake failure in the automobile, do not greatly mitigate the individual's responsibility to stop at the intersection. Sociological analyses of the conditions under which one is allowed to claim he is ill, that is, allowed to take the role of the sick person, show that illness is under the continuous appraisal of responsible persons such as an employer, a spouse, or a parent for possible malingering and illustrate in microcosm the operation of group control over possible false claims of disability when poor motivation is the real cause.

Perhaps another reason for the *a priori* assumption that deviance is motivational in nature is that it places the blame on the individual for his behavior, rather than on society. If a person confronts his society with a claim of ignorance or poor ability, it reflects on the adequacy of his prior socialization, which is society's responsibility. Motivational deviance, in contrast, is less easily attributable to defects in society's socialization process and is more easily viewed as being the individual's own fault.

The burden of proof thus is placed upon the actor to show that his motives are pure. The demand that he do so is from society's viewpoint legitimate, since it is difficult to distinguish ignorance or lack of ability from hypocritical claims either that one did not know what the rules really were, or that he was unable to live up to them.

This view of human behavior may benefit society, but there is a price for using this approach in the resocialization of deviant persons. The treatment of deviance would be more effective if it made use of techniques which accord with the reasons for behavior: where ignorance is the cause, education; where lack of ability is the difficulty, improved training; where motivation is the problem, a planned and deliberately executed program of manipulation of rewards and punishments to reorient the individual to appropriate goals and behavior.

If deviance comes from ignorance or lack of ability and yet punishment is administered in the mistaken idea that motivation is the cause, a frequent result is the individual's rejection of the values of society which he formerly accepted. The child who wants to get good marks in school but cannot do so because he needs glasses and is unable to study without them soon learns to hate school if he is punished for his failure to achieve good marks. Similarly, the child from a lower-class home who does not understand the ways of the school or his classroom and is ignorant of much of what is expected of him soon learns to dislike school if he is punished by the teacher for his nonconforming behavior. Treatment of a case of deviance arising from ignorance or lack of ability as if it springs from the wrong motives actually may produce the more serious situation of deviant motivation, the very problem that society is trying to eliminate.

Now, as to the life cycle, motivational deviance in infants and younger children is more readily tolerated. What is more, children, more often than adults, are allowed to claim ignorance or lack of ability as the cause of nonconforming behavior. The concern with motivation, and the requirement of proof for motivational purity, are less evident in the early stages of the life span. Once again, this is true both of the informal family systems and, at least in our society, of the courts of law. Probably the reason is that there is time to train the child, and the socializing agencies remain in firm control of adequate rewards and punishments to influence the course of his interests. With each advancing year, however, instances of deviant motivation are viewed with more seriousness, and the child's responsibility for motivational conformity increases in accord with the age-graded developmental schemes which are accepted in his culture, until the full-scale responsibilities of adulthood are demanded of him.

When Resocialization Fails

What happens when resocialization efforts directed to the control of deviance prove to be ineffective, that is, when deviance continues? One important result is that the social system is broken as the deviant individuals withdraw from the groups in which they are involved. A married couple may become divorced; a student may drop out of college; a man may change his job; a wife may insist that her family move from one neighborhood to another. Sometimes this withdrawal is anticipatory, and the individual never does participate in significant groups in society but lives in a marginal position; the bachelor and the recluse are cases in point. In its extreme form the dissolution of the system sees the deviant individual leaving his society to form a separate one with like-minded people. The establishment of utopian communities is one such phenomenon; emigration of groups to a different country is another; in more complex societies the establishment within them of small, subcultural groups of deviants tolerated by the society, such as hobos or enclaves of disaffected adolescents, is a case in point.

But in many instances the system is not or cannot be broken; two other solutions to the continued existence of deviance may then appear [see Parsons (25)]. One is a continuation of the social system under conditions of stress. The system continues in operation with one or more members being deviant in their actions. Evidently the balance of rewards and punishments gained from participation in the system as a whole by its members makes it possible to tolerate the deviance of a minority in one or another area. There would be, of course, a continuing effort to exercise control over the deviant persons. This system, in comparison to systems without deviance, should be characterized by greater hostility, mistrust, and fear of dissolution because of its precarious nature. Most important, perhaps, would be the need for each member to control his antagonism toward the misbehavior of others so as not to destroy the social relationship. This requirement causes even more suppression of feelings.

The other solution to continuing a system with a deviant member (or members) is to alter the expectations in such a way as to eliminate the deviance. The expectations of others in the system are changed to accord with the formerly deviant actor's performance or objectives. The definition of what is deviant has been changed, and the new behavior or values accepted. Attempts to resocialize are abandoned, and others acquiesce to the deviant individual's wishes. The individual has transformed the system, the rebel has won his cause, the innovative aspects of his behavior have been accepted and legitimized, and the socializing agency has been forced to reconsider its objectives.

How does the handling of continued deviance in a social system differ for children and adults? First, the parent-child relationship is hard for the child to break. Formerly it was easier for the deviant child to escape by running away, but today in our society he is locked into the system by a number of child welfare laws. Thus children more often than adults are socialized in systems that they cannot leave.

The resolution of the problem of deviance in the groups to which the child belongs therefore must take one of the other two forms noted above. The deviance may continue and be tolerated by the system. If so, then the child, more frequently than adults, has his major socializing experiences in interpersonal systems characterized by considerably greater hostility, depth of feeling, and range of affect, and more productive of repression in personality.

Alternatively, the child's groups, especially the family system, may change in the direction of his desires so as to redefine the deviant case as acceptable. At first one thinks of the adult as being the more autonomous, mature member of society with clearly greater power to change the behavior of those with whom he interacts. He may alter his marital relationship, change his boss's ideas, and influence the community's political climate. But on reflection it is clear that the child also may influence the family system in which he lives. He modifies the expectations of his parents about his wishes and actions, teaching them the concept of age-grading and of developmental tasks, forcing them to convert both their proscriptions of what he should not do and their demands for what he should do to fit his own maturational sequence (8). The eldest child especially serves as a revolutionary force; subsequently each child alters the family system to conform to his own desires, although rarely as radically as did the first.

*   *   *   *   *

In closing we have reached the intersection of the two great interests in the study of personality and social structure: how society manages to socialize the individual so that the work of society gets done, and how individuals manage gradually to transform the social system in which they live. The deviant person who cannot be resocialized is the source of innovation and change in the behavior and ideals of society. The fundamental problem to be solved by an enduring society is to train individuals to be responsible, and yet provide for the development of the free and creative person. A middle way must be taken between producing the undersocialized and the oversocialized person. A society must develop members who conform and fit into the existing order, as well as those who, although deviant now, are better equipped to live in the world to come. Social responsibility has been the concern of this work. Freedom, creativity, and revolution properly are the topics of a separate work.

BIBLIOGRAPHY

1. Becker, Howard S., Blanche Geer, Everett C. Hughes, and Anselm Strauss, *Boys in White: Student Culture in Medical School,* Chicago, Illinois: University of Chicago Press, 1961.
2. Becker, Howard S., *Outsiders,* Glencoe, Illinois: The Free Press, 1963.
3. Becker, Howard S., "Personal Change in Adult Life," *Sociometry,* Vol. XXVII, No. 1, 1964, pp. 40–53.
4. Becker, Wesley C., "Consequences of Different Kinds of Parental Discipline," in *Review of Child Development Research,* Vol. 1, New York: Russell Sage Foundation, 1964.
5. Benedict, Ruth, "Continuities and Discontinuities in Cultural Conditioning," in *A Study of Interpersonal Relations,* Edited by Patrick Mullahy, New York: Heritage Press, 1949, pp. 297–308.
6. Borgatta, Edgar F., Leonard S. Cottrell, Jr., and Henry J. Meyer, "On the Dimensions of Group Behavior," *Sociometry,* Vol. XIX, No. 4, 1956.
7. Brim, Orville G., Jr., "The Parent-Child Relation as a Social System: I. Parent and Child Roles," *Child Development,* 1957, Vol. 28, No. 3. pp. 345–346.
8. Brim, Orville G., Jr., *Education for Child Rearing,* New York: Russell Sage Foundation, 1959.
9. Brim, Orville G., Jr., David C. Glass, David E. Lavin, and Norman Goodman, *Personality and Decision Processes:* Studies in the Social Psychology of Thinking, Stanford, California: Stanford University Press, 1962.
10. Caldwell, Bettye M., "The Usefulness of the Critical Period Hypothesis in the Study of Filiative Behavior," *Merrill-Palmer Quarterly,* Vol. 8, No. 4, October, 1962.
11. Clausen, John A., and Judith R. Williams, "Sociological Correlates of Child Behavior," in *Child Psychology:* The Sixty-Second Yearbook of the National Society for the Study of Education, Part I, Chicago, Illinois: University of Chicago Press, 1963, Chapter II.
12. Glick, Paul C., *American Families,* New York: John Wiley, 1957.
13. Goffman, Erving, *Asylums,* Garden City, New York: Anchor Books, Doubleday, 1961.
14. Goodman, Norman, "Communication and the Self-Image," Ph.D. Dissertation, New York University, New York City, 1963.
15. Inkeles, Alex, "Sociology and Psychology," in *Psychology:* A Study of a Science, Vol. 6, Edited by S. Koch, New York: McGraw-Hill, 1963, pp. 317–387.

16. Kelley, R. H., "Two Functions of Reference Groups," in *Readings in Social Psychology*, Edited by G. E. Swanson, T. M. Newcomb, and E. L. Hartley, New York: Holt, 1952, pp. 410–414.

17. Kemper, Theodore D., "The Relationship Between Self-Concept and the Characteristics and Expectations of Significant Others," Ph.D. Dissertation, New York University, New York City, 1963.

18. Kluckhohn, Florence, "Dominant and Variant Value Orientation," in *Personality in Nature, Society, and Culture*, Edited by C. Kluckhohn and H. A. Murray, Revised and Enlarged Edition, New York: Knopf, 1953, pp. 342–357.

19. LeVine, Robert, "Political Socialization and Culture Change," in *Old Societies and New States*, Edited by Clifford Geertz, Glencoe, Illinois: The Free Press, 1963, pp. 280–303.

20. Linton, Ralph, *The Cultural Background of Personality*, New York: Appleton-Century-Crofts, 1945.

21. Maccoby, Eleanor E., "The Choice of Variables in the Study of Socialization," *Sociometry*, Vol. 24, No. 4, December, 1961.

22. Merton, Robert K., "Contributions to the Theory of Reference Group Behavior" (with Alice S. Rossi) and "Continuities in the Theory of Reference Groups and Social Structure," in *Social Theory and Social Structure*, Revised and Enlarged Edition, Glencoe, Illinois: The Free Press, 1957, pp. 225–281.

23. Merton, Robert K., "Social Structure and Anomie" and "Continuities in the Theory of Social Structure and Anomie," in *Social Theory and Social Structure*, Revised and Enlarged Edition, Glencoe, Illinois: The Free Press, 1957, pp. 131–161.

24. Neugarten, Bernice L., "Personality Changes during the Adult Years," in *Psychological Background of Adult Education*, Edited by Raymond G. Kuhlen, Chicago: Center for the Study of Liberal Education for Adults, 1963, pp. 43–76.

25. Parsons, Talcott, *The Social System*, Glencoe, Illinois: The Free Press, 1951.

26. Parsons, Talcott, "Family Structure and the Socialization of the Child," in *Family, Socialization and Interaction Process*, Edited by Talcott Parsons and Robert F. Bales, Glencoe, Illinois: The Free Press, 1955.

27. Sewell, William H., "Some Recent Developments in Socialization Theory and Research," in *The Annals of the American Academy of Political and Social Science*, Philadelphia, Vol. 349, September, 1963, pp. 163–181.

28. Sherif, M., *An Outline of Social Psychology*, Revised Edition, New York: Harper, 1956.

29. Vincent, Clark E., "Socialization Data in Research on Young Marriers," in *Acta Sociologica*, Vol. 8, August, 1964.

30. Wilson, R. N., "The American Poet: A Role Investigation," Ph.D. Dissertation, Harvard University, Cambridge, Mass., 1952.
31. Wrong, Dennis H., "The Oversocialized Conception of Man in Modern Sociology," *American Sociological Review*, Vol. 26, No. 2, April, 1961, pp. 183–193.

The Structure of
Formally Organized
Socialization Settings

STANTON WHEELER

M ANY people spend much of their lives in organizations whose explicit mandate is to change them. One is expected to learn basic skills in a school, to get advanced training in universities, to recover from psychosis in a mental hospital, to be exposed to corrective programs in prisons, or to learn special work skills in trade schools. Thus socialization processes are not restricted to those that occur within the intimate environs of the family or other closely knit networks. Increasingly, they are a function of large-scale bureaucratic organizations. Our lives from age five or six to age twenty or so, and often intermittently thereafter, are bound up with large-scale organizations where new learning or relearning is expected to take place.

The aim of this work is to identify and discuss the attributes of these organizations that are likely to lead to different socialization outcomes for persons who pass through them. The focus is on the organizational context of socialization and on the way in which differently organized settings may produce different socialization experiences. This focus draws upon two related areas of broader sociological inquiry, one suggested by the concept of socialization, the other by the concept of organizational analysis.

The heart of the essay lies at the intersection of these two concerns, although of necessity it deals with only a small portion of the problems and interests they suggest. Unlike most studies of socialization, little attention will be devoted to the analysis of individual differences in response to socialization pressures, or to the attempts at immediate interpersonal influence by those serving as agents of socialization. These important concerns have been reviewed elsewhere and will receive little attention here (45). The emphasis in-

stead is on features of the social context within which the more immediate processes occur. The justification for this emphasis is simply
that these features are an important but little-studied part of the
socialization experience. Just as individuals may become differently
socialized because of differences in past experience, motivations, and
capacities, so may they become differently socialized because of
differences in the structure of the social settings in which they interact. It will be my aim to clarify the nature of those settings.

The guiding assumption is simply that in many situations individuals remain highly adaptable and flexible, prepared to fit their behavior into the demands of the current social context. The result is
that we must not look only at underlying motives, that is, at how
people have internalized deeply rooted features of the social order.
Much can also be learned about the process of socialization by tak-
ing a close look at the structures and situations within which it occurs (4).

Similarly, organizational analysis includes much that we will omit.
The emphasis in this essay is on features *distinctive* of organizations
that process people. Thus there will be much said about how recruits are brought into the organization and about their passage
through it, but little about the standard variables of organizational
analysis, such as size, degree of decentralization of authority, and
staff-line relations. Of course, much that occurs in what we are calling the people-processing or socializing organization is common to
all formal organizations and therefore needs no special review.
This work focuses specifically and directly on settings where some
people are formally charged with the task of influencing others so
that the others will leave the setting with different skills, attitudes,
values, or other qualities from those with which they entered.

Until recently, there was little need for discussion of the variables
common to all organizations that process people and in terms of
which such organizations may vary. Most studies were based upon
single-case analyses, where the organizational as distinct from individual variables were in effect held constant. At best there were
studies of two or three organizations, and then often within the
same concrete type of setting such as the prison, manufacturing
plant, or school. The growth in funds, technology, and indeed in
conception of social organizations now permits the study of a variety

of settings within the same research project, and it thus becomes appropriate to focus upon the organizational features that may vary systematically across the different settings.

Throughout, reference will made to socializing agents or agencies. These are the persons who, acting on behalf of the organization, are expected to train, educate, modify, mold, or in other ways change the individuals who enter it. We will use the concept of socializing agent even though the person in question may not realize (as one reader put it) that he is "in that line of work." But there is no similarly general term for referring to the person who is supposed to be changed—no general word to encompass the patient, student, trainee, or inmate. We will simply use the term *recruit* to refer to the person who enters the organization and is expected to change. The organization within which both agent and recruit interact is a socializing organization or agency.

There are five sections. The first clarifies the general properties of organizations that process people by examining typologies in which such organizations can be located. The aim is to distinguish socializing organizations from closely related types of setting. The next three sections discuss the variables which differentiate among socializing organizations and which are likely, therefore, to lead to different socialization outcomes. These might be thought of as independent variables likely to produce variations in outcome. One of these three is devoted to organizational goals and internal structure, another to the recruits' patterns of movement through the organizations, and a third to the relation between the organization and the broader society. The concluding section briefly comments on some gaps and further problems, and specifically on the need for sociological theories of socialization outcomes.

SOME PROBLEMS OF CLASSIFICATION

One way to identify the important qualities of a particular class of phenomena is to examine the implicit classification systems within which the class can be meaningfully located. This procedure can help sharpen the boundaries between related concepts, thus clarifying the structure of the particular class under consideration. Typically the class under study can be located meaningfully in more than one typology or classification system. This seems especially true of the class being considered here: namely, organizations designed to socialize people. A principal reason is that the defining properties of such organizations are likely to have different degrees of relevance depending on whether the agent or the recruit is the focal point for analysis, no matter how much the system of relations between the two is stressed as the common element. Thus it is useful to locate the organizations that process people in two different typologies. The first is more relevant to the processing agency; the second, to those who are ostensibly being socialized.

A Typology of Processing Systems

Organizations that process people are part of a broader typology of systems within which things are processed. The characteristics common to all members of the typology include some more or less clearly defined point of entry for the thing that is to be produced, some notion of movement through a series of stages or steps, and finally some point of exit from the system. In all cases, the product that leaves the system is expected to be different from that of entry. It may be different because a new organization has been put on parts that entered as separate pieces, as in the assembly line production of an automobile. Or it may be different because something new has been added to an already formed product, as when a bald tire is recapped or when a person attains new knowledge or skills. The important point is that work is done on whatever entered in the hope that its state will be changed when it leaves.

One dimension crucial for understanding such processing systems is the degree of differentiation of the processing agency. At one pole are systems where a single task is performed by an individual. At the other pole are highly differentiated systems, where many specialized tasks are allocated to different individuals or groups. The distinction between degrees of differentiation includes related indicators of complexity such as the sheer size of the organization, the number of separate steps or stages in the process, and the degree to which other elements of bureaucratic structure are present, but it will suffice here to treat all these as elements of differentiation.

Another dimension is the character of what is processed, an important attribute being whether it is a social or a nonsocial object. The primary distinction is between people and things, though this is a distinction too crude for certain instances. For example, a hospital processes people, but usually at the level of the physical anatomy and hence would be classed here as working on a nonsocial object. Where the primary purpose is to change the knowledge, beliefs, attitudes, or skills of those who pass through the system, the work is focused on a social object. The distinction between a nonsocial and a social object, as applied to persons, is roughly similar to that between the biological organism and the personality (40).

A simple typology of processing systems, resulting from cross-classifying the two dimensions of degree of differentiation and type of product, yields the fourfold pattern indicated below. Type I is illustrated by the individual craftsman or the family production system. The mass production factory is the best concrete illustration of type II. Type III is exemplified by any dyadic socialization pair: teacher-pupil, mother-child, doctor-patient. When the complex bureaucracy of type II is joined by the processing of people, as in type III, the result is type IV, the socializing organization: the school, prison, mental hospital, or trade-training center.

A Typology of Processing Systems

		Degree of Differentiation of Processing Agency	
		Relatively Undifferentiated	Relatively Differentiated
Type of Product	Nonsocial Object	Type I Individual craftsman	Type II Mass-production factory
	Social Object	Type III Teacher-pupil Mother-child Doctor-patient	Type IV School, prison, mental hospital, trade training center

Perhaps the most important difference in the movement from physical to social objects is that people can talk back. Unlike the inanimate object, the person on a production line can respond to his environment and often significantly alter it. He may agree to go along with the program, or he may fight it. His own goals may be at vari-

ance with those of the socializing agent. Therefore the whole set of
"human relations skills" may have to be brought into play by the
agent to accomplish the task at hand. Furthermore, the person is
likely to have ties outside the immediate processing system that may
exert further pressure on the socializing agents in the system. The
influence of youthful peer groups on parents' socialization efforts
with their children is a familiar example.

It is when both these movements—from a relatively undifferentiated system toward a highly differentiated one, and from a nonsocial
product to a social one—are joined to form an organization that processes people, that the specific qualities relevant to the study of such
settings emerge most clearly. Unlike the simple, often dyadic socialization process, new demands are introduced by the broader organizational form. Now it is not simply one person who can talk back.
There emerges a chance for those being socialized together in the
mass production process to communicate with each other and establish a social force in the organization not found in the typical manufacturing concern. In addition to whatever problems of communication and social control the organization faces from its lower echelon
staff, it is confronted with similar problems from the very units
being processed. As a consequence those in the lower echelons of
the official system face problems found only at higher levels in the
typical factory. The lower operatives in industry are spared the
problems of role conflict faced by their superiors, the foremen. But
in organizations that process people these conflicts are generated
throughout the system, for all employees are in the middle. This
heightens problems of communication and role conflict.

The typical dyadic model of socialization in relatively undifferentiated systems may be carried over into the more complex organizational form. In fact, it usually is, as when tutor and pupil are transformed into teacher and student, or therapist and client in a psychiatrist's office become therapist and patient in a hospital. But three
new problems are also generated that may significantly alter the
relationship between the members of the dyad. First, even though
the dyadic relation may remain, it now takes place in a complex organization, and new problems of scheduling and coordination arise.
Whereas in the simpler state the agent may have had to handle
a number of problems seemingly remote from his primary function,

the organization may provide new differentiated units that relieve him of these responsibilities. Bookkeeping departments, attendance offices, and appointment secretaries are examples of forms that remove responsibilities the agent may have carried in less differentiated systems. Theoretically, these may free him for concentration on the socialization task, but there are other forms of control required by the mass production system that may offset these benefits. His work must now be coordinated in time and space with that of others, and there are features of the setting that must hold for all members despite individual differences in wants, desires, and tastes. Economy may dictate, for example, the quantity ordering of materials such as books, calculators, or other necessary equipment, thus reducing individual autonomy. All these differences are similar in kind to those brought about by the movement toward formal organizations in processing physical objects. They stem from the effort to accomplish just what was done in the simpler and less differentiated system, but to do it more efficiently.

The second problem emerges with the realization that recruits may be influenced in fundamentally new ways by utilizing the organization itself as a mechanism of change. Now it is no longer simply a question of doing more efficiently what was previously done, but of gaining new leverage and a greater range of effects than was possible in the simpler systems. Perhaps the clearest instance has been in therapeutic settings, where the use of group therapy, first justified as a simple expedient to cope with large numbers, came to be seen as having new potentials for effecting personality change. Later, when concern emerged about "the other twenty-three hours," the total organization was viewed as a major factor in rehabilitation (34). This trend leads directly to a search for organizational variables that may produce differences in outcomes for recruits.

Third, these changes raise new potentialities and new problems for the recruits. Although they may perhaps receive more specialized and differentiated training, now both they and the organization face problems of integrating the diverse programs and assuring that the proper balance and fusion results from the influence of separate parts.

Although we are concerned with only one kind of processing system in this work, it is relevant to ask about the conditions under which the various types occur and their consequences for the broader systems in which they are embedded. It seems obvious, for example, that it was not until most of the material problems of survival were solved, and men freed from physical labor by development of an industrial technology, that energies began to be turned in great amounts to the development of occupations and professions for the processing of people. There are still large differences in the extent to which such processing is organized in large bureaucracies. Comparison of the size and other indicators of scale of schools, mental hospitals, and prisons in different societies might suggest some of the conditions leading to differing rates of bureaucratization of the socializing organizations.

A Typology of Interpersonal Settings

When a person moves into a new interpersonal setting, a major problem he faces is understanding the setting and coming to terms with its demands. He must develop a workable "definition of the situation" to guide his action. In addition to whatever definition he derives from his background, much of his orientation can be expected to come from what he learns about the setting itself. The socializing agents will have their version of this process, but since he is a recruit and they are not, his position will be different.

A primary feature of the setting that may aid the recruit in developing a meaningful definition of it is the extent to which others in the setting are or have been in his position and can aid his adaptation. An aspect of this is simply whether he is facing the new setting alone or in the company of others. This can be called simply the *individual* or *collective* status of recruits. As Becker (4) and others have clearly noted, much adult socialization is organized so that a large number of persons are introduced to the new setting simultaneously—a group or class is the target of socialization. Under these circumstances adaptation is likely to proceed much differently from the case where one person enters alone, since the recruits can arrive at a collective solution to the problems they face.

A second and related aspect is whether the recruit has been preceded by others who have been through the same process and who can teach him about the setting. This might be called a *serial* pattern of socialization, to distinguish it from *disjunctive* patterns wherein the recruits are not following in the footsteps of predecessors.

The definition of these two aspects is arbitrary. For example, the number of recruits entering simultaneously may be more important than the simple dichotomy of individual versus collective entry, although studies of individual conformity in the face of social pressure suggest that the presence of just one more like-minded person may radically alter responses (1). The meaning of entering a setting together is also not precise. Individuals may enter the setting at different times, but at intervals small enough that they are thought of as a unit and are "processed" together.

A Typology of Interpersonal Settings

		Social Context of Entering Members	
		Individual	Collective
Social Composition of Other Members	Disjunctive	**Type I** Oldest child in family; first occupant of newly created job	**Type II** Summer traning institute; group of visiting scholars in foreign country
	Serial	**Type III** New occupant of a job previously occupied by another person	**Type IV** Schools; universities; professional training centers (approximated by prisons and mental hospitals)

There is similar arbitrariness in the distinction between disjunctive and serial patterns of socialization. For example, even if there are no persons in the setting who have preceded the recruit in his specific position, persons in similar organizations may have done so, and he may attempt to learn from them.

Combining these two characteristics—the individual or collective status of recruits, and the serial or disjunctive character of the setting—results in a fourfold typology arranging socialization settings by the extent to which others therein can help the recruit arrive at a workable definition of his situation. The prototype for the indi-

vidual-disjunctive pattern (Type I) is the oldest child in a family or
the first occupant of a newly created job. The collective-disjunctive
pattern (Type II) is illustrated by a summer training institute or a
group of scholars visiting a particular country in a certain year.
Type III, the individual-serial pattern, is frequent in occupational
recruitment: the individual is the only one occupying his position,
but others have filled it before him and have moved on to other positions in the organization. Finally, the collective-serial pattern typi-
fies large-scale organizations such as schools, universities, and professional training centers and is approximated by prisons and mental
hospitals.

To explore the conditions and consequences of each of the four
types more thoroughly, consider the two cases in which each influence works separately. In the first, the individual can turn to persons
still in the setting who formerly occupied his position, but not to
others who are experiencing it with him. In the second case he can
turn only to the latter. The first case seems generally more conservative from the the point of view of the organization, since earlier oc-
cupants of the position may accumulate, test, and subsequently dis-
card many possible solutions, and since its members can speak to the
new recruit with whatever authority seniority and experience offer.
It is anticipated that he may look to them for guidance in problem
solving, leading to a patterned transmission of the organization's culture to new members.

In the second case, labeled the collective-disjunctive type, these
influences are missing, but the individual is not thrown solely on his
own resources. Since he faces the problems along with others, they
may work out a collective solution. The recruits who accompany
him can still use past experience, but it is likely to be less relevant,
coming as it does from their own backgrounds. The emergent collective solution or style of response is likely to be less stable and predictable than in the individual-serial pattern. The pressures to find a
joint solution will probably be unusually great, since there can be no
reliance on the stability provided by "older, wiser heads."

The serial pattern, precisely because of its stability, risks stagna-
tion and is likely to be undesirable from the point of view of agents
when things are going badly. There is the likelihood that the former
recruits will train the new ones using the defeating pattern. Should
morale be low, older members introduce the newer ones into the

low-morale system. Should lower-level persons be disrupting the program, they are likely to attempt to indoctrinate the new recruits with their viewpoint. Thus, when organizational staff try to get it out of its current rut or to develop novel solutions to problems, they are likely to move toward the disjunctive pattern precisely because of the potent socializing effects of the serial pattern.

An illustration of this process is provided by an innovation in prison and correctional programs. When California's Chino prison was constructed as a model institution demonstrating the best modern penal philosophy, its founders refused to hire any correctional staff who had worked in prisons before, and they took great care in selecting new inmates for the program, with the aim of making a break with an older correctional philosophy. The common-sense observation is that the first class "sets the tone" for future recruits.

The distinction between a serial and a disjunctive pattern may be applied both to the socializing agents and to the recruits or clients, as well as to the higher and lower echelons of the organization in question. Only when a new organization is getting under way, or when there has been a general "house cleaning," will all or most of the participants be in the disjunctive pattern. Frequently, all or most recruits will be in the serial pattern: college students follow others, as do college faculty members. But often a pattern is serial from the point of view of the socializing agents, yet disjunctive from the point of view of the recruit. This is true wherever there is a position to be filled by only one person, whose predecessor leaves before the new appointment is made. Under these conditions, the socializing agents will have some performance norms to apply to the person, deriving from judgments of his predecessors. Since the recruit was not there when the other person was, he lacks this knowledge. Some of the problems this situation creates are suggested in studies of *succession* in organizations (30).

Occasionally this process is reversed, and the persons ostensibly being socialized build up a knowledge from long-term experience that is likely to be greater than that of those who are to socialize them. This seems true in some prisons and mental hospitals, where staff turnover may equal or in some instances exceed inmate turnover. It is not surprising in such circumstances that the organizations are sometimes literally run by the inmates. This is one of the characteristics that distinguish prisons and mental hospitals from most educational settings, where the possibility of a recruit becoming a "lifer" is more remote.*

The collective patterns, as Becker has noted, may provide the recruit with support, should he care to resist the efforts of the socializing agents to change his beliefs, attitudes, or behavior. Where initial commitment is low, as it is among recruits to correctional settings, the collective nature of the process contains the seeds of counter-revolution or at least of a socializing process opposed to that of the staff. Prison is perhaps the most familiar example of how a collective pattern may function to protect recruits from symbolic and actual "pains of imprisonment" (48). It appears to get force both from its serial character, with older inmates providing informal socialization for the newer recruits, and also from its collective nature, with inmates typically being processed in cohorts, as determined by similarity in dates of arrival.

Collective patterns may make a more positive contribution under certain circumstances. If initial commitment to the organization and its recruits is high, the peer group may be harnessed as an aid in socialization, thus intensifying the effects of the formal socialization program. Shil's observations (46) on primary groups in the army and the common feeling in graduate schools that students may learn from each other as much as or more than they do from the faculty are instances of this intensifying effect.

It may be that the collective settings yield quite successful or quite unsuccessful socialization outcomes, depending on the initial commitment and the degree of organization among recruits. This is presumably the reason why personnel in organizations like prisons stress that their recruits should establish individual adaptations, go it alone, mind their own affairs, and have little to do with other inmates, while the agents in colleges and universities encourage student interaction as a meaningful and important part of socialization.

Initial commitment is of course only one of the characteristics that will help determine whether recruits accept or reject the official aims of the organization. The manner in which the staff members work with the recruits and the immediate pressures of the situation, as

---

* It is interesting to note, however, the concern of university graduate departments about "perpetual" graduate students, the imposition of regulations aimed at forcing such students to obtain an advanced degree within a fixed interval of time or else leave the department, and the role of such students in some of the recent collective demonstrations on university campuses.

well as the recruits' initial commitments, will influence the collective response. In some medical schools, for example, despite high initial commitment, the recruits may organize in ways the staff does not approve (5, 7). Conservative administrators in any type of socialization setting may encourage individual adaptations for fear that the organized recruits may move in unacceptable directions.

Since isolated, individual adaptation seems to go against the usual tendency of persons to desire knowledge about their new setting and companionship while in it, we might expect this pattern to be chosen only under rather special circumstances. Those modes of socialization or resocialization that we think of as most extreme and that have as their goal not a mere change in the skill level or the attitude of the person being socialized but rather a thorough reconstruction of his personality typically involve an individual and disjunctive pattern. A prime example is psychoanalysis. In some cases other recruits may be present but are used to destroy prior patterns rather than to sustain them, to build mutual mistrust rather than action in concert. Examples are brainwashing and thought-reform programs. Indeed, in a recent analysis of radical individual change, McHugh argues that such destructive conditions are necessary before new patterns can be established (39).

The conditions for use of an individual disjunctive pattern are not restricted to radical resocialization. Organizations are likely to create a new position when novel and creative programs are desired. The person entering such a position may be left free to define his role as he sees fit, becoming, in effect, his own socializing agent. And of course these conditions are likely to be personally attractive to those who wish autonomy and the freedom to follow their own paths.

It should be clear that the typology refers to the possibility, rather than the actuality, of interpersonal contacts. Those entering a collective-serial pattern may spend most of their time with persons who have been in the setting longer, or they may spend it with those who entered with them. The conditions and consequences of adopting one or another pattern are not often studied. Wallace's (50) recent study of socialization in colleges shows the potent effect of the serial pattern, even when other alternatives are available. And of course some individuals may remain effectively alone in any setting if they fail to establish ties to other members.

Interesting questions can be raised about the relative frequency of occurrence of the four types. It seems clear that they are not found in equal numbers. Collective-disjunctive patterns, for example, occur fairly rarely. Most collective settings have been programed to have a serial character as well. With industrialization and related institutional processes, the need for mass socialization has led to an increase in the serial-collective patterns relative to others.

Relation to Other Typologies and Concepts

These two typologies present different ways of locating formally organized socialization settings, one calling attention to the general features of processing systems, the other to the possible interpersonal contexts found when the objects processed are human beings. In each case there is one type (Type IV) that tends to be filled by the same concrete social settings. It is the dimensions of variation within those settings that are under consideration. It should be remembered, however, that the distinctions are analytic and that some of the concrete illustrations merge with the other defined types. Prisons and mental hospitals, for example, have all the serial processing qualities noted for schools. Their collective character is a little different, however, since they are continually receiving and releasing recruits, while dates of reception and exit are much more routinized for schools.

Socialization types can, of course, be classified and reclassified in an infinite variety of ways, and much heated verbal argument may ensue about the most appropriate dimensions and labels to be attached to them. The typologies which have been presented earlier must be justified by their ability to clarify the distinctive characteristics of organizations that process people and by suggesting relevant studies that will help inform a comparative analysis of interpersonal situations. It is suggested, for example, that organizations that process people will differ in important ways from those that process things, that within the people-producing variety important differences turn on the complexity of the processing system, and that from the point of view of recruits a critical feature is the extent to which they are accompanied or preceded by others similarly situated.

Different features could have been chosen as bases of classification: whether the recruits are voluntary participants, whether the settings approximate a total institution or community, or any of the variety of dimensions along which social settings can vary. These alternatives were neglected in part because they are already familiar, in part because the dimensions used here help illumine features that are often neglected because they are so obvious. But it may be useful to identify briefly the points of overlap with other typologies and concepts.

Etzioni's classification (21), for example, is based on the nature of the authority and compliance system in the organization and is not sensitive to differences in the type of product. The "lower-level participants" in Etzioni's scheme are sometimes employees of the organization (workers on an assembly line), sometimes persons being processed by the organization (students, patients, inmates). The distinction between these two categories of participant is crucial for the present discussion.

Most socializing organizations would appear in Blau's and Scott's typology as service organizations, that is, organizations in which the prime beneficiary is the client in direct contact with the organization (12). But some socializing organizations might be found in Blau's and Scott's category of commonweal organizations, since the organizations were established to benefit the public. Many organizations that service clients would not appear as socializing organizations. More generally, organizations that merely provide a service (such as shops, dental clinics, or legal aid bureaus) and have no long-range plans for systematic changes in their clients would not qualify as socializing. A recent paper by Bidwell and Vreeland (10) draws distinctions somewhat similar to those introduced in this work and by Blau and Scott.

Parsons' classification, based upon the primary function the organization serves for the broader social system, would unite many of the socializing institutions with religious and other organizations on the grounds that both serve the function of pattern maintenance —the provision for cultural continuity across generations. Some others, such as mental hospitals and correctional agencies, would be classified with courts and other structures that serve integrative functions (41).

Lastly, the concept of the socializing organization is closely linked to that of the total institution, as described in the definitive work by Erving Goffman (28). Many of the ideas expressed later owe a debt to Goffman's treatment. His distinctive emphasis is on the encapsulation of the individual by the establishment; the chief defining property is that the organization is set up as a 24-hour living establishment for its inmates. That some total organizations attempt to change their recruits whereas others do not is of only peripheral interest in Goffman's scheme. It becomes a central interest here. But whether or not the system is "total" in Goffman's sense is not a defining property of the socializing organization.

The two conceptualizations share the binary quality noted so clearly in Goffman's analysis; the distinction between keepers and kept is paralleled by that between socializing agent and recruit. But beyond that, the prime emphasis in the study of socialization is on the problematic relation between what is being taught and what is being learned.

Developmental Socialization and Resocialization

The focus of the remainder of this study will be on sources of variation within the class of organizations that process people. Instead of using a typological framework, the major variables will be simply introduced and discussed serially. However, the common-sense division between schools, colleges, and universities on the one hand, and mental hospitals and prisons on the other, is important enough for special attention.

Schools and universities are familiar examples of what might be called *developmental* socialization systems, where the formal purpose is the training, education, or more generally the further socialization of the individuals passing through. These are the organizations we recognize as legitimate for persons to move through, though not everyone is expected to do so. Contrasting to the developmental socialization systems are what we might call *resocialization* systems, where the formal purpose is to make up for or correct some deficiency in earlier socialization.* These are largely the organizations designed to resocialize the deviant, in contrast to those designed for the further socialization of conventional persons.

This simple distinction is so pervasive that it becomes useful for

---

* A paper prepared for the Social Science Research Council Conference by Yonina Talmon makes useful further distinctions among types of resocialization that this paper passes by.

discussing variations in the structure of socialization patterns, especially since the two types are likely to fall at different ends of any
dimension along which the patterns vary. Both types are clearly dis-
tinguished from those where the prime purpose is merely to hold or
detain individuals, with no formally stated mission to bring about
personal change. This distinction, like the others mentioned above,
is analytic. A specific prison or mental hospital may appear more
developmental, and some schools may take on the character of prisons. This is entirely consistent with the argument drawn here, since
the intent is to locate dimensions that apply across the range of concrete instances. It is to be expected that the most benign therapeutic
community in an open prison might be less prison-like than, say, a
prep school organized along military lines. Indeed, when we locate
these organizations by their positions on some theoretically meaningful continua there may be good reason for challenging the official
labels by which they are known.

ORGANIZATIONAL GOALS AND SOCIAL STRUCTURE

Socializing agencies are like other formal organizations in having
a rich and complex social structure. There appear to be several
different aspects of their internal order that are likely to influence
socialization outcomes.

Organizational Goals

Formal organizations are often defined as systems for the achievement of explicit goals. There would be no reason to call special attention to problems of goal definition and attainment in socializing
organizations were it not that the definition of goals emerges as a
distinctive problem so frequently in such organizations. Everett
Hughes (31) has put it well:

> Compared to the restrictions, resistances and distortions of purpose,
> assignments, and efforts in a school, a mental hospital, a social agency
> or a prison, the much studied restriction of production in the factory is
> simplicity itself. In the factory, there is at least fair consensus about
> what the object produced shall be. There is often no such consensus in
> institutions where things are done for or to people. (p. 76)

There are important differences both within and among socializing organizations in the specificity or generality of the goals set for

members. Bidwell (9) has referred to this as a distinction between role socialization and status socialization. By role socialization Bidwell means the training and preparation for performance of specific tasks, and by status socialization he refers to a broader pattern of training designed to prepare the recruit to occupy a generalized status in life with its associated life styles. Training in engineering, typing, or forestry is largely training in role socialization; training in the liberal arts (except for those who are to become liberal arts teachers) is an example of status socialization, preparing the recruit with some of the general background necessary to enact the status of college graduate.* In resocialization settings, vocational or educational training programs and the learning of specific trades are examples of role socialization, whereas participation in counseling, guidance, and spiritual or moral training sessions are examples of status socialization.

Often these two types of goals are seen as complementary, and effective socialization is assumed to involve movement toward both. Sometimes dynamic causal relations are presumed to exist between the two types. Much of the recent theory of adolescent delinquency, for example, uses such a distinction: youths who fail to get adequate vocational training and opportunities—who are limited, in other words, in their opportunities for adequate role socialization—develop a moral outlook, value system, and life style that take the form of a delinquent subculture. In this instance, the presence or absence of relatively specific skills opens or closes paths to more generalized social statuses.

Socializing organizations that contain both types of goals are likely to develop two different staff systems, one concerned largely with role socialization, the other with status socialization. Though persons at the top of such organizations may see no conflict between

---

* Zelda Gamson has noted in a personal communication that the split between engineering and hard sciences on the one hand, and liberal arts on the other, also reflects a difference in the extent to which they aim at resocialization. At the college she studied, the liberal arts program included strong efforts at changing the student's identifications, interests, and commitments, and did not confine itself to the more narrowly conceived program of training that she found in the natural science programs. This difference led to important differences in the ways the various programs responded to students. See her "Social Control and Modification: A Study of Responses to Students in a Small Non-Residential College," Doctoral Dissertation in Social Psychology, Harvard University, 1965.

the two systems, they are frequently competing for scarce resources and there is likely to be a certain degree of estrangement between their members. In the treatment-oriented prison, for example, workshop and vocational supervisors may have their programs interrupted by a psychiatrist's schedule of individual or group counseling. One consequence for recruits in such systems is that they may be exposed to conflicting images of the purposes of the organization, with one staff grouping subtly devaluating the work of another.

Socialization and resocialization settings also differ markedly in how far the goals are oriented to the adequate socialization of the new member or to the maintenance of the social system in which he was once located. In developmental settings, agents are likely to see one of these as the equivalent of the other: if a medical student gets good training, it will help his career and contribute to the health and welfare of society as well. Resocialization settings, however, are typically faced with a conflict over this since the recruit is there because he needs resocialization, but also because he constitutes "trouble" for the external world. His length of stay and his situation while there are based both on an estimate of his resocialization needs and on an estimate of the amount of trouble he caused. The two are not necessarily highly correlated. Resocialization systems are unusually subject to this conflict in goals, and many of their standard features, such as a clear distinction between the custody and the treatment staffs, result from it. These systems may also differ in the specificity of their goals, with resulting difficulties of assessment where the aims are diffuse (17).

Since the goals of socializing organizations are typically also goals for their recruits, special problems are raised about participation in goal setting and the meshing of the recruits' objectives with those of the organization. Such organizations lack the generalized medium of exchange provided by money in most other production organizations. The staff of a mental hospital wants the patient to recover his mental health; the patient wants to get out of the hospital. Teachers wish their students to seek general knowledge; the student wants to pass examinations and get a degree. Socializing organizations apparently differ greatly in the extent of meshing of the goals, and also in how far recruits are allowed to participate in the determination of goals. But it is important to differentiate between participation in setting individual goals within the structure of the organization, and participation in establishing the goals and policies of the organization itself. Almost all high schools and colleges, for example, allow some flexibility in course programs for individual students, under the title of elective subjects. Some colleges, however, allow the students a wide range of participation in collegiate decision-making, whereas others permit only a pseudo-democratic show of participation and decision-making in trivial issues. A sense of participation may be particularly important in settings that effectively cut the recruit off from other means of involvement. One would predict, for example, that the effectiveness of socialization would vary more with the degree of participation in goal setting in institutions that are relatively "total" than in those that less effectively seal off the recruits' participation in other spheres.

Thus the organizations that process people may differ widely in (a) the degree to which there is differential emphasis on or a clear separation between role socialization and status socialization, (b) the extent of conflict that is felt between the needs of the recruits and the needs of the external community, (c) the development of separate organizational hierarchies that give expression to these two differences, and (d) the extent to which recruits participate in the setting of goals and the adequacy of the fit between the goals of the recruits and the goals of the organization. These differences ought to have an important effect on the total socialization process in a wide variety of situations.

Variability in Composition of the Recruit Population

At a general level, there is at least one quality that all recruits to a particular organization have in common: the basis for their recruitment. All prison inmates have been committed by an adjudicating agency, all new entrants to professional schools have wanted for some reason to apply, and so forth. There are likely to be other ways in which recruits are similar, and still different ways in which they may vary from one another. It is the combination of these two that provides much of the flavor and quality of interaction in the settings. Public schools, for example, have students who are roughly similar in age, similar in marital status in that almost all are single, and similar in residence since they must live in the immediate community.

But the students differ in sex and in socioeconomic status, so the latter two dimensions become important bases of variability. Prisons, on the other hand, have precisely the reverse pattern. They are typically single-sex institutions or have separate and highly segregated facilities. They are likely to draw almost all their inmates from lower social classes. But their inmates may differ widely in age, may come from all sections of the state (or of the country in federal institutions in the United States), and may contain a large proportion of men who are either married or divorced. So while social class and sex serve as broad organizing features of schools and many other developmental systems, age and marital status loom as more important in resocialization systems, especially prisons.

Because of these differences, the clients and socializing agents in resocialization systems are faced with radically different circumstances from those confronting their counterparts in schools and colleges. The variance in age and therefore in life-cycle position seems particularly important. Youthful inmates of 20 may be exposed to what may be either a steadying or a depressing influence on their immediate adjustment and future aspirations. Faced with 70-year-old men who have lived most of their lives in institutions, or with married men who are worried about their wives' fidelity or who are receiving divorce papers, they may encounter reasons for developing a fatalistic attitude toward the future, quite apart from whatever component of a criminal value system they find around them.

This is merely to underline, then, that variance in some of the gross and superficial characteristics of the recruit population may have direct implications for the sorts of socializing experiences the new recruits will encounter. Because these characteristics are such obvious features of the different organizations that process people, their effects are perhaps too frequently glossed over or unnoticed.

Interaction Rates

Some organizations allow much opportunity for their recruits to interact with staff. Others tend to isolate the recruit so that he has little contact with the socializing agents. Similarly, in some settings recruits are quite free to interact with their fellows, while in others they are prevented from interacting by timing, the program, or enforced restraints. While the amount of contact the recruit has with either the socializing agents or other recruits is partly a matter of his choice (and that of the agent), it is also influenced in important ways by the social ecology of the organization. It is the latter feature that is important for this discussion.

Part of the interaction pattern is determined by the sheer numbers in the various categories. Student-faculty ratios, like inmate-staff ratios, give some indication of the opportunity for meaningful interchange between socializing agent and recruit. Both developmental and resocializing organizations apparently pride themselves on achieving low ratios of recruits to agents, for a low ratio makes possible, at least theoretically, a greater impact of agent on recruit. Temporal patterns are of course also important, and recruits in appropriate locations may have more than usual access to the socializing agents. The role of the inmate "politician" is a good example. He typically is assigned to a position such as a clerk for a staff member, or as barber in the staff barbershop, which provides great opportunity for staff contact and perhaps personal influence.

Patterns of interaction among recruits depend on similar conditions. Students who live off campus or at home, like inmates who are confined in single as opposed to congregate cells, may find little opportunity for the establishment of enduring social bonds with their peers. In a study of Scandinavian prisons we have found great variability in the sheer amount of time available to inmates for interaction with their fellows. In some institutions, designed many generations ago according to the isolation ideology of the nineteenth century, inmates are still housed in separate cells, fed individually in their own rooms, and in other ways kept isolated. In other institutions designed to meet a newer correctional ideology, these conditions are not found. Rates of friendship formation are highly correlated with these features of ecological structure and program. It is important to note that these physical features, like many others in different situations, are not based on a current official ideology. Rather, they are the legacy of the past, too permanent and costly to be easily removed to fit the different present.

These dimensions of interaction and its ecological base are of course found in all organizations. They would require no special mention here were it not for their heightened importance in organizations designed to change people. We would not expect the rate of change to be independent of the rate of interaction with significant elements of the setting. Indeed, Maccoby (38) has noted that child-rearing studies infrequently focus on the sheer amount of interaction between parent and child, though the amount may be at least as important an influence on socialization as the particular style of interaction. Similarly, there are relatively few studies that use the interaction rates as a variable *across* socialization situations, so it is difficult to assess the importance of these gross characteristics for the socialization process.

Role Differentiation and the Formation of Subcultures

One of the most important effects of all three of the problems just discussed—organizational goals, variance in group composition, and interaction rates—is that these conditions influence the formation of subcultures and informal social roles among the recruits. In other words, they set the conditions in which the rich informal life of socializing organizations may operate.

Such organizations usually have a relatively undifferentiated mass of recruits. A factory-type production system suggests some similarity in the objects produced. Customarily there is some formal ranking and differentiation, based to some extent on time in the system or on the specific formal program being undertaken by the recruit. Thus juniors and seniors may be allowed privileges not extended to freshmen and sophomores, one's major field of study provides some basis for formal differentiation, and so on. In resocializing organizations, perhaps the most typical formal differentiation is by custody assignments, some patients or inmates being placed in open wards or allowed to work outside the confines of the institution, while others must remain within.

Often, however, the differentiation built into the formal structure is not enough. First, it seems to require too gross an orientation. To the extent that meaningful interaction occurs among the recruits, it appears necessary to provide a mode of organizing responses to the recruits that falls in between treating each as a unique case, and treating all alike save for the minimal formal differentiations. Second, the problems of recruits differ from those of agents, but it is primarily the problems of the latter that define the formal pattern of differentiation. Therefore we might expect to find informal patterns of differentiation among the recruits organized around their problems, and giving expression to issues that may be irrelevant from the perspective of agents.

It is here that the concept of *social types* becomes so important in these organizations. This concept refers to the placing of recruits into categories along with associated labels that express something about each category. The concept of social types is of course applicable in many other settings and is indeed one of the principal ways by which large informal systems become structured (36). It seems especially prevalent in the larger socializing organizations, where mass-production tendencies provide few formal status distinctions among the recruits. It is important to note that the social typing emerges from the recruits themselves; the concept does not refer to analytical types or typologies which the investigator may use to make sense of the community or organization he is studying. The social types are usually defined by differential responses to the problems found in the organization. The need to make the responses of other recruits predictable is one of the chief forces underlying the tendency toward social typing. The social typing system enables one to think in terms that are not immediately dictated by the observables of dress or formal status.

Examples of social typing systems abound in both college and university life and in prisons. On college campuses, the wonk, the grind, the jock, the campus politician, and various other types suggest something of the systematic variety of orientations to the college on the part of its students. Certain combinations of these orientations can be seen as defining subcultures that provide a generalized mode of response to the college environment. An intriguing typology of such subcultures has been described in detail by Clark and Trow (15). A variety of orientations is also found in prisons and is symbolized by the use of special labels that catch the dominant theme of the response of particular types of inmates to their setting. Schrag (44) and Sykes (48) have described such typologies of orientations, and a thorough review of prison typologies has been provided by Gibbons (27). The women's prison also exhibits a clear social typology (25).

This is not the place for a full description of the various types. The important thing is to identify the underlying themes. The typing systems, for example, are usually highly responsive to the dominant themes and needs of the recruits, which in turn depend upon how the organization is structured. The social types recognized by students on college campuses and embodied in the description of collegiate subcultures lay stress on involvement with ideas and on attachment to the college or university as an institution. The types found in prisons typically give little emphasis to the role of ideas, but much to loyalty relations and to varieties of relatedness to staff and to inmates. Thus it would be expected that the dimensions underlying the social types would depend upon the specific conditions confronting recruits. A common element likely to flow through all such typologies, however, is some expression of authority relations and response to them. Thus the collegiate bookworm who submits to the demands of the formal system is similar to the conventionally oriented inmate or the teacher's pet in grammar school. The theme of attachment or alienation to the authorities seems to pervade social typologies.

Often, however, the assignment or choice of concrete persons for the various roles is related to their external statuses—to properties they bring in from the external world. The person's previous social activity and career prepare him better to fulfill one rather than another role in the informal structure. To draw again from the prison instance, customarily, those inmates who are defined as "square johns," that is, who go along with the administration and remain relatively aloof from other inmates, are those who have no prior criminal record, who often have committed offenses under the press of extreme situations, and who have little in common with many of the prisoners. Those who most closely embody the stereotyped norms of the inmate world have typically been involved with group crimes, especially property offenses, over a long period of time and come from high delinquency areas of our major cities.

Becker and Geer (6) have used the concept "latent culture" to refer to a culture having its origin and supports outside the setting in which the members are currently participating. To the extent persons share a similar latent culture, it may become operative in their current situation. It is clearly distinct from the manifest culture, that is, the culture that arises in response to the immediate problems faced by members in the setting. In socializing organizations, the distinction refers to the relative contribution of the internal setting versus the external world in providing a basis for whatever common or differentiated culture appears. Becker and Geer argue that latent culture will operate when there is high variability of input into the setting, and where the press of the immediate situation is not so strong as to prevent the penetration of external roles. Yet even where recruits face a common set of problems to which they must adapt or adjust, the solutions to those problems are likely to vary, and this variation will probably be related to the earlier experience of the recruits.

The impact of latent identities is surely not independent of organizational goals or the possibilities of interaction in the system. Authorities in some organizations aim for what might be called *homogenizing* settings that tend to reduce the relevance of prior experience for present adjustment. In others, which might be called *differentiating* settings, authorities may urge recruits to give expression to the different backgrounds and interests they bring into the organization.

The intended effect of the stripping and mortifying processes found in many total institutions is precisely to reduce the effect of a person's past on his present. Organizations that emphasize the varied programs available for their recruits may want to work toward an intensifying or differentiating effect, stressing the individual differences in background that recruits bring with them. These differences are most readily noticed in the mass or individualized processing of recruits and in the symbols of dress, appearance, and conduct that are stressed. We may expect an intended homogenizing effect in organizations where men must all wear identical clothing, have their hair cut the same way, and show similar posture and bearing. These are the qualities that distinguish army training units, military academies, and some private and parochial schools (20). The other extreme is usually found in those colleges where students are free to dress as they please, to take many electives and few required courses, and so on. It is under these circumstances that special subcultures seem most likely to form.

Even within a category of organization there may be much variation. In the study of Scandinavian prisons, we find that old-style custodial prisons tend toward the homogenizing type where it is difficult to predict a man's present attitude from knowledge of his background. But the institutions for youthful offenders tend to show strong relationships between an assortment of background characteristics and current attitudes. Apparently the crucial intervening variable is the amount of free interaction time, that is, the amount of time during which inmates are allowed to associate with their peers. Where the time is restricted, as in the older custodial prisons, there is little opportunity for like-minded inmates to locate each other, talk, and therefore perhaps reinforce the effect of their past upon their present. In the newer and more open settings assortive processes operate freely, and there is a higher correlation between what a man once was and what he feels about his present situation.

Thus there is evidence that informal differentiation and the development of social types and subcultures occur wherever large numbers of people are placed in roughly the same formal status categories. The nature of the subcultural systems that form always bears some relation to immediate problems of adjustment to the situation. The system of social types and subcultures gives expression to variations in solutions to these common problems. The extent of proliferation of subcultural forms depends on (a) the extent to which the organization fosters or encourages diverse responses, which in turn is reflected in (b) the potentials for forming cliques and other meaningful interactive groups. These in turn are likely to give expression to the latent cultural identities imported into the system by recruits.

The Setting and the External Environment

Patterns of subcultural differentiation constitute only one of a number of ways in which recruits are affected by external ties. Important dimensions also include the ecological tie between the setting and the external community, the transfer of knowledge from the community into the organization, and the place of the organization as a whole in the motivational structures of recruits. Each of these features deserves attention.

Some settings are removed from on-going social contexts; others are caught up in them. The type case in colleges is the private campus in rural Vermont versus the streetcar university in a major urban area. Some prisons, despite walls, bars, and wire, are located in the center of large cities that produce much of the criminal population, thus making it easy for family members and others to visit. Others are located far from the centers of population. The extreme in this regard is the Federal Reformatory for Women in Alderson, West Virginia. Since there are few women prisoners, there are few institutions for women and Alderson (the major federal women's prison) houses female offenders from all over the country. Consequently there is an extremely low rate of visitation from relatives and friends (25).

One might ask about the optimal degree of separation for various purposes, and about the conditions under which organizations will try to maximize or minimize their separation from other social settings. The intensity of any socializing experience is probably related to the degree of separation, for separated settings are able to reduce potentially conflicting influences. They can command more of the recruit's time and energies. However, there is a problem of balance, for if the goal of the organization is to provide training or inculcate values that may be useful after the person leaves it, too much separation may breed highly unrealistic images, and severe "reality shock" may result. The greater the separation, the greater the segregation of contexts and therefore the less carry-over or generalization value from what is learned. One way to attempt a resolution is to provide trial periods for the learner in the external world, followed by a return to the socializing organization for a review of the experience. Examples include the work program for students in colleges like Antioch and the granting of furloughs to inmates in resocialization settings.

Where recruits have little access to events in the external community, either because of the location of their organization or because of restrictions on leaving it, important functions are performed by the novices who enter. Although they are new, they are the ones who have most recently been in the community to which some of the members will return. The new recruit may trade his information about the outside for information about the inside which the older recruit can offer. In prisons, for example, the newest recruit may be sought out by others from his community to find out about people and affairs there. He may know whether a friend is in trouble, whether a girl friend is running around with someone else, whether police policies on narcotics arrests have changed, and so on. This gives the new recruit in resocialization settings a status he frequently lacks in developmental ones, where he is being prepared to enter a new status rather than to return to a former one.

A further aspect of ties to the external system has to do with the basis for negotiating a contract with the socializing organization. One could ask about any setting: does a member's commitment or adjustment to it depend on developments within the setting itself or on developments in the external environment? The question concerns the place of the organization in the life of its members. This location seems to depend upon many things, including the degree of ecological separation, the extent of initial commitment, and the length of time members expect to be in the organization. There appear to be large differences in the capacity of the organization to engage its recruits so that their reactions are a function of events within it. The contrast between elite private colleges and "open-door" community colleges seems great in this regard.

There are important differences even within a specific type of socializing organization. Irwin and Cressey (32) have noted, for example, that understanding of inmate culture in prisons requires a clear distinction between the "thief" subculture, where there is neither interest in nor identification with life inside the institution, and the "convict" subculture, where inmates are thoroughly enmeshed in the political and personal intrigues of institutional life. Among those oriented to the external world, strong changes in reaction within the setting may be dependent upon changes outside. For example, some inmates give up their plans for a conventional career when they learn of the death of a relative, the filing of divorce papers on the part of a wife, and so on. To the extent that the recruit's orientation depends upon external contingencies, the organization must develop ways of handling these problems, as well as those that are a function of its internal structure.

The Concept of Social Climate

Opposed to the forces that make for diversity in response to socializing organizations, is a countertendency to perceive this system as a whole: agents, recruits, and the social, emotional, and ecological world in which they live tend to get caught up in an over-all assessment. The concept of social climate calls attention to this and refers to the over-all "feeling tone" about the setting. Perceptions of the social climate may of course differ, depending upon one's position in the system, and assertions about some tendency toward a specific state or feeling tone need to be buttressed by evidence. However, it is common to find some central theme.

The concept of distinctiveness is relevant. Clark and Trow (15) have noted that some colleges and universities develop historically in such a manner that they have clearly separable identities from any other institutions of higher learning, with traditions, values, and norms that differentiate them from other outwardly comparable places. It is perhaps a commentary on resocialization settings that they are seldom remembered for these distinctive qualities.

A frequent source of the social climate is the predominance of a specific recruit subculture. Thus the subcultures denoted in the Clark and Trow report are not distributed evenly through all colleges. At large state universities, where a collegiate culture predominates, the whole campus may be thought of largely in terms of football and other athletic activities.

In most social climates, however, the dominant theme focuses on authority relations between socializing agents and recruits. What the agents assume about the recruits and vice versa tends to establish the emotional tone of the organization. From the early studies of Lewin, Lippitt, and White (37) on democratic, authoritarian, and laissez-faire climates, through Gouldner's (30) analysis of representative and punishment-centered bureaucracies, to the pressing concerns for liberal values on a college campus or a therapeutic orientation among staffs in mental hospitals, the concept of social climate expresses something about the feelings generated by the total set of relations between staff and recruits. Relations may be warm, free, and easy, or harsh and hostile. Both within and between the major social categories there may be a feeling of trust or of suspicion and lack of confidence.

Unlike most of the previous categories, the concept of social climate refers to a subjective, attitudinal set rather than a condition effectively known by studying interaction patterns or personal characteristics. It is thus harder to pin down. Yet it seems crucial to an understanding of organizations that process people, especially since the dominant social climate tends to symbolize so many different concrete elements in the setting. Indeed, variations in social climate presumably flow from some of the other variations described above and are consequential for individual participants in each organization, even where their personal stance is at odds with that of the dominant climate. The social climate is a prime example of the possible effect of social context on socialization processes.

MOVEMENT THROUGH THE STRUCTURE

The previous section dealt with attributes of organizations that could be assessed at a single point in time—the sorts of characteristics that might be studied in cross-sectional analyses of organizations. We now turn to features especially crucial to organizations that process people, since they refer to the process of movement through the setting.

Anticipatory Socialization

Most persons are introduced to a new organization only after they have had time to think about it and develop some perspective. A practical question facing most agencies of socialization is how to manage the advance preparation so as to increase the probability of successful outcome. Just as the first class of recruits to a new program may set the tone, so the initial adaptation and adjustment of a new recruit may influence his future career in the organization.

Socialization settings differ markedly both in their capacity and in their efforts to manage this process. They vary in their power to select the recruit population, in the amount of advance preparation they require of the recruit, in the amount of time that intervenes between selection for the organization and actual participation in it, and in their capacity to control the sources of prior knowledge about the organization.

Developmental systems can sometimes afford the luxury of controlled intake. Also, they may select their recruits long before they actually arrive, thus allowing time for each to prepare for the other. Entry to private colleges provides a good example, many students being selected in the spring for their entry in the autumn. During the intervening time they may talk to others about what the college is like, read books they know will be assigned during their first few months, and in other ways prepare to participate in the new environment. (A more extreme example is the enrollment of children for private elementary and preparatory schools years before their actual entry.) Where the agencies know who they will receive, special

plans can be adopted to maximize the impact on the recruit, for example, the arrangement of rooming assignments in residential colleges.

Since much activity may go on between the decision to enter a
program and actual participation, it seems likely that a considerable
amount of the socialization effect is achieved before the person enters. While it would be a mistake to assume this as a general princi-
ple, it is noteworthy that there are few studies of this pre-entry
period. Studies showing no change in opinions or attitudes during
the course of participation in a socializing organization might lead
one to conclude that there was no effect. However, another possibility is that there were strong effects, so strong, indeed, that most prospective recruits changed before participation.

In some developmental organizations and most remedial ones,
there is less power of selection, less opportunity for advance preparation, a shorter time period between selection and participation,
and less power to influence the source of whatever presocializing
experiences the recruit will receive. Most of these features add up to
a high degree of shock and difficulty for recruits during the period
of entry. Goffman's analysis (28) of the process of entry into a mental hospital suggests in detail the impact the process may have on
the person being resocialized.

What is not so often stressed, though still important, is that the
resocialization agency also suffers from the irregularity of entry procedures. Unlike most developmental agencies, it cannot schedule its
arrivals for a particular day or month but must frequently be prepared to receive them at any time of day or night. The rate of intake
may vary widely from day to day or month to month, in part because of the problematic character of deviant behavior, in part because of such a chance occurrence as the illness of a Superior Court
Judge or several judges being on vacation at the same time, producing a "backlog" which they discharge upon returning to work. Unlike most schools and training programs, the "intake" rhythm of prisons and mental hospitals is set by other agencies, typically ones
which are not in position to see the effects of their decisions on
either the inmate or the staff. In this respect they they are similar to
emergency operations like those performed in hospitals and disaster
areas.

Just as the organizations that process people differ widely in their control over entry, so the recruits themselves show much individual variation in their preparation. Some come from backgrounds that provide much preparation, either programed or unplanned. Others have little. Boys from gangs in high-delinquency areas who are committed to institutions are in about the same position as are youths from select prep schools who enter elite private colleges and universities. In its own way, each group will be prepared to take the new environment in stride. They will have friends and acquaintances who have preceded them, and a belief that the event was going to happen some time anyway. In contrast, both the middle-class offender and the outstanding student from a small rural high school may be quite unprepared for the moves into their respective new institutions. The critical variable seems to be the extent to which the prospective recruit has access to peers who have been through the same process.

It is useful in analyzing the sources of knowledge about the organizations to consider the ratio of the knowledge that comes from the official agents to that coming from peers. Initial adjustment is probably an inverse function of that ratio. The individuals most shocked will be those whose anticipations have been guided by the conventional adult world. The least shocked will be those who have been guided by their peers. This is logical because the socializing agents have good reason to present an idealized version and because they simply are not in a position to view the process from the recruit's standpoint. Peers may err also, but they are likely to have the sort of information that the prospective recruit wants and needs to get along.

Entry Procedures

Organizations that process people vary widely in the extent and range of their formal programs for new recruits. Almost all such organizations have some sort of guided tour or information exchange so that recruits can learn their way around, and the agents can size up the recruits. Where entry is voluntary, the recruit may have to register or in other ways make a record of his agreement to participate; where entrance is involuntary, the same process occurs, though persons other than the recruit may sign the relevant documents. But some programs go further in providing orientation lectures describing the ideology of the organization and other more formal indoctrination procedures. They place the new recruit in a formal status as a learner and provide programs designed to ensure his commitment to the organization and its purposes, and to instruct him so that he can participate fully and knowingly in the organization's activities. Other organizations provide little in the way of formal socialization programs; the recruit's initial learning is left mostly to chance.

Two circumstances are likely to lead to the socializing agents viewing commitment to the organization as problematic. First, if they can assume that the recruits are there to "get the most" out of their experience, they may be able to forego a formal indoctrination process, but if they cannot assume this level of commitment, they are likely to think it necessary to develop special programs to guide and direct their recruits. Second, formal orientation programs may also be called for where the organization's program constitutes an essentially new and different procedure for its recruits.

On both these counts, developmental organizations usually differ sharply from resocialization settings. First, since commitment to organizational objectives cannot be assumed in most resocialization organizations, it is probable that special orientation and indoctrination programs will be considered necessary. One consequence of foregoing an indoctrination program is that the recruit is free to choose his socializing agents. Without an indoctrination program, the prison inmate may look to the administration, the treatment staff, the guards, or other inmates for relevant information. The same alternatives are at least nominally open to the staff, though in both cases the simple ecology of institutional life may lead to one source becoming more important than another. Especially during the early stages of membership, the socialization process is not likely to be left solely to the amorphous effects of the environment and its members and to the chance affiliations that may develop. When the recruit is placed in the formal role of learner, that status-placement includes an assumption about whom he should look to for appropriate models. Perhaps a major reason for introducing formal indoctrination programs, apart from the learning of bits of information or ideology, is to establish one segment of the organization as the legitimate and appropriate socializing agency.

Second, agents in developmental settings are able to benefit from the recruit's prior experience in similar settings. After all, he has been going to school since kindergarten, he has encountered teachers before, and he knows what education is all about. Resocialization settings are, however, an essentially new experience for many of their clients. Thus one might expect that prisons and other types of resocializing centers, to the extent that they are concerned with goals other than custody, would invest relatively more of their resources in reception programs than would colleges or universities.

The Amount and Sources of Knowledge about Recruits

Only certain portions of the socialization program are typically required of all recruits. Other parts are presumed to be relevant to or needed by only a segment of the recruit population. Once there is a commitment to a differentiated program, there must be some mechanism for allocating persons to the various alternatives. Just as recruits need an orientation to the socialization setting, so do members of the organization require knowledge about the recruit.

In developmental organizations, the recruit typically is allowed to participate in making the choice among the available alternatives. Supervisors or counselors may be provided to aid him in making his choice, but even here his guidance and proper placement may be assured by considering only a few aspects of his background known to be relevant to his performance,—often whether he is bright enough, has learned enough before entry, and is motivated. Since he is allowed to make the choice and is assumed competent to do so, there is no need to build a full dossier on his background, achievements, and failures. Whatever need there is for such information typically is met during the selection process, rather than when he is on the scene. In the selection process, there is typically a systematic bias in the information brought to the attention of the socializing agency. An important part of the selection often depends on letters of recommendation, and frequently the recruit himself may pick his references. Persons who have reason to doubt his competence, who are privy to information about his misdeeds, are typically not solicited for references. Among those who are solicited, there is usually an understandable effort to present the recruit in the best possible light.

Thus the information that begins to accumulate, to the degree that it includes description of his past, is likely to be biased toward a favorable or optimistic view of the recruit. The socializing organization is not likely to be made systematically aware of any blemishes in the person's past. If the individual has some difficulty while in the socializing organization, it may well appear as an isolated incident in an otherwise unruffled career. Any bias in the information made available to the organization about the recruit is in the direction of emphasizing the positive rather then the negative.

These situations are quite different in resocialization settings. There, since the recruit has failed in some way before entry, he is usually deemed incapable of making wise decisions about his program. These are more often made for him by the socializing agents, who are thus required to build up a fund of knowledge about the recruit that exceeds the necessities in developmental organizations. Whereas the latter usually assume that the criteria for success are relatively few, clear, and specific, resocializing agencies typically find many and diffuse reasons for the recruit's past failure.

Specifically, success is likely to be seen as the result of ability or prior training in areas relevant to the training task faced by the agency, while failure is more readily viewed as some basic maladjustment that encompasses the whole personality. The agency must understand that failure in order to recommend the appropriate program for the recruit's benefit. In the search for that understanding the individual's past is likely to be revealed in full and stark detail. Letters may be written to all educational, welfare, police, and court agencies in the vicinity of the recruit's residence, requesting pertinent information. If he has lived in a city with highly professionalized and bureaucratic welfare and judicial facilities where good records are kept, there will be detailed accounts of his childhood, his school record, his family's contacts with court and welfare agencies, community psychiatric facilities, and the like. These provide ample basis for reconstructing the recruit's career as a series of failures. Should he have difficulty in the organization, it can be seen in his case as part of a broader pattern and not an isolated incident. The many self-defining properties of this flow of information are examined in detail for the mental hospital case by Goffman (28).

The importance of these differences between developmental and resocializing agencies is that, to the degree that they depart from an objective picture of the recruit, they are likely to move in opposite directions, one revealing an excess of what are usually construed as favorable qualities, the other an excess of unfavorable ones. To the extent that this happens, the organization itself may be molding the future careers of the recruits in unintended ways.

Again, it is important to remember that concrete instances of people-processing organizations may be quite unlike the "ideal type" of developmental or resocializing organization. To the extent that current programs in the schools, for example, call for systematic contacts with the guidance counselor, personality as well as IQ testing, special programs for the early spotting of the underachiever or the delinquent, the schools are involved in resocialization functions. Questions of the quantity and quality of information available in the files of different types of socializing organizations remain to be answered by empirical research. This dimension may be more of a product than a condition of different socialization environments, but in any event it would seem fruitful to include it in studies designed to tap differentials in the socialization process.

The Fate of Role Failures

A related feature of the composition of the recruit population has to do with the fate of role failures. Here there is another obvious and important difference between socializing and resocializing organizations. Developmental organizations get rid of their *failures*. They flunk, are expelled, or drop out. Resocialization settings frequently get rid of their *successes*. The failures are kept longer or else are returned. Thus the longer a recruit remains in a developmental organization, the more likely he is to have interaction with those who are succeeding. The failures are removed from immediate visibility.

Precisely the reverse occurs in many resocialization settings. There, the recruit is continually reminded of failure by the presence of so many failures around him—the long-term psychotic, the habitual offender, and so on. Typically it is only these failures who are in a position to tell him what it is like to be back in the community. Quite naturally they are a biased source of information. These procedures of handling role failures would seem, on the surface at least, to further complicate the task of resocialization in mass organizational settings.

If enough persons fall into the category of the highly successful or the highly unsuccessful, special programs may be set up within a given type of socializing organization that have the effect of further intensifying the experience. A familiar case is the "blackboard jungle" phenomenon or, at the other extreme, the special programs for highly motivated and gifted children. Since there will be variability in the talents, skills, or other relevant traits among the population of recruits, any sizable program will be faced with the problem of mixing the various elements. This is the problem of "ability grouping" in the schools, "criminality grouping" in the prisons, and more generally the problem of compositional effects for which models of analysis have been worked out by Davis (19). Whether these programs have the intended effect is an empirical question just beginning to be investigated in any detail.

The diverse ways of handling those who fail within a given program are extremely important in evaluation of outcomes and in the way in which the socializing agents may come to think about their organizations. If programs are judged by the later conduct of recruits who leave through routine channels, it is useful to get rid of the more doubtful cases during the socializing process. The measured success of the program is achieved at the cost of having little impact, or perhaps a negative one, on those it excludes. Where the organization is literally the last stop—the most escape-proof prison, the locked back ward of the mental hospital, the school that receives all the disciplinary cases from the other schools—then the staff may have a built-in rationale for failure that is difficult to overcome by morale-boosting programs. Not the least of the consequences is that whatever power resides in the negative sanction of threatened expulsion of the recruit is no longer available to the staff as a means of social control (48). Efforts to sustain a rehabilitative philosophy may fade in the face of security problems.

Time and Timing

One of the defining features of socializing organizations is that recruits are expected to leave as well as to enter. But the organizations differ in the average length of stay of their recruits, in the variance in the length of stay, and in the certainty or uncertainty of the length of stay at various phases of movement through the settings. Each of these features of time is worthy of brief comment, since each appears to enter in important ways into the fabric of formally organized socialization environments.

A reason for calling attention to the average length of stay as an important variable in socialization programs is that so little is known about it. Studies have, of course, been done that relate length of stay to "outcome" in prisons and mental hospitals, but these typically yield data on individual differences rather than on differences that characterize the systems as a whole (24). Yet we might expect that the length of the program or stay that is typical for the organization as a whole will have its impact on those who move through it.

One suggested effect of a lengthy stay is the formation of a strong and cohesive culture among the recruits. Where the average stay is short, there may be little opportunity to build up a stable social order, especially to establish symbols to which the recruits become committed. Thus we might expect four-year colleges to have a more stable student social structure than two-year junior colleges, and similarly for prisons or mental hospitals where the average stay is long.

Another effect of the average length of program is its capacity to serve as a quantitative indicator of what persons in the program have gone through or accomplished. Sometimes the length of program combines with the length of preparation to enter it to serve this function. Prestige may be accorded members of professions, not simply because of the special skills and expertise assumed to emerge from training, but from the sheer length of the program itself. Indeed, agents typically have a conception of the optimum amount of time to be spent in the organization and are likely to be upset if a recruit is seen as moving too fast or too slowly, even though he is meeting all the technical requirements. Concern for these problems, for example, is frequently evident in graduate schools.

The variance in length of stay for recruits is likely to be an important feature of the organizatcon. Where the variance is low, recruits can more easily see themselves as "in the same boat," for their fates are similar and time itself cannot loom as a major differentiating characteristic. But a high variance belies the assumption that the recruits are much alike and deserving the same sort of program. A high variance in length of stay invites the question, "Why does he get to remain longer than I do?" or "Why must I remain longer than others?"

One of the important consequences of the movement to convert holding places for deviants into resocialization settings is that variance in length of stay has apparently increased in such settings. The trend toward "individualized justice" in correctional institutions and individualized treatment in mental hospitals makes distinctions among the recruits as to their resocialization needs and hence, frequently, the length of time they remain. Especially since such resocialization organizations are not customarily thought of as desirable places to be, much of the talk among recruits is likely to focus on the justice or injustice in the handling of "time" by the organization. In developmental organizations, which usually presume a more normal and typical process of movement, these matters of time are more routinely programed, and the variance in stay is typically small.

Where the variance is small, there is usually great certainty regarding length of stay, since all will have the same expected period. Increasing the variance does not necessarily increase the indefiniteness. In the historical development of time and sentencing procedures in prisons, for example, the movement has been from relatively undifferentiated sentence lengths, through highly differentiated lengths where the sentences were definite and could not be changed, to highly differentiated sentences with the possibility of review by the sentencing agency or members of the agency, so that conduct *after* arrival in the setting could be used as evidence about the appropriate length of stay. It was only the most recent move, the one that enabled sentences to be revised depending on the inmate's progress in the institution, that introduced a systematic uncertainty about time.

The problematic character of deviant behavior means that uncertainty about time is more likely to characterize resocialization than developmental organizations. The requisites for completing programs in the two types differ radically in specificity, from a detailed statement of the number of hours of credit of such and such a type required for completion of most educational programs, to the diffuse requirement to "get well" found in mental hospitals. Just as the effects of varying lengths of stay are little known, so are there questions about the effect of the uncertainty of length of stay. Patients having illnesses for which speed of recovery is highly variable, such as tuberculosis, expend much effort trying to reduce the uncertainty (42).

It seems clear that the recruit's concern and anxiety about when he can leave the resocialization organization may take his energies away from the problem that confronts him as it is defined by the agents. For these reasons there are those who argue that it is better to give a recruit a prescribed length of stay and to release him at its end no matter what his state, thus removing this strain. But such a policy runs counter to many individualized care and treatment models.*

Exit Procedures

The period when the recruit leaves the socialization organization is likely to be marked by special programs or ceremonies, just as was his entry. But again, different organizations follow widely varying patterns about what transpires during this period. Although anticipatory socialization may occur spontaneously (22, 51) if the program has been intensive or if it has effectively encapsulated the life of the person during his movement through it, special procedures may be felt necessary to prepare him for his exit—the equivalent of a decompression or recompression chamber. This is typically a period when the individual is expected to learn how to operate outside without the direct aid and support of members of the organization. Prerelease units or halfway houses fit the model. It seems significant that colleges and universities have few such programs, partially, one assumes, because they lack some of the features of most total institutions and hence have not so completely removed the person from his participation in wider spheres.

A second type of activity near the end of the stay consists of various rituals and ceremonies announcing the successful completion of the socialization experience. Such ceremonies often provide a suc-

* In the Danish prison system there are two psychiatrically oriented institutions in which the directors differ in their assumptions about the effect of uncertainty. In one, inmates are given definite expectations as to when they will leave; in the other they are not. It would be interesting to study systematically the differences in the responses of inmates in the two situations.

cessful sealing off of the experience of membership, the accomplish-
ment being symbolized by a formal certificate, diploma, or degree.
The obvious case is graduation from high school or college. More
generally, it seems that in developmental organizations much more
symbolic display is associated with leaving than with entry. The
rites of passage on the way out are more clearly demarked than
those of entry. Furthermore, it is a collective celebration, a segment
of the recruit population going through it together, with all that this
implies for the "collective conscience."

In resocialization settings, however, whatever ceremony is present
is likely to precede entry rather than exit and is usually defama-
tory in character if not in intent. Indeed, the reverse of the status-
elevation ceremonies associated with leaving schools is what Garfinkel has described as the status-degradation ceremony (23). It
is interesting that for persons committed to prisons the official, ceremonial, and public degradation that is symbolized by the commitment procedure is not systematically reversed when the individual
returns to society. When he leaves, it may indeed be with official
blessing, but there are no greetings by a welcoming committee, no
special efforts at reintegration, save those provided by the staff in
connection with prerelease programs and planning. The individual
typically leaves alone rather than in company with his peers among
the recruits. Whatever welcome he receives on arrival at his home
destination is left solely up to his relatives and other primary ties.
Although the community, through the court or other official agency,
formally withdrew its support of the individual through its commitment action, there is no symbolic or ceremonial action by the community to restore the definition of the person that obtained before
the initial actions.*

This is not to say that such ceremonies would be helpful from the
recruit's standpoint. Conceivably the identification and publicity at-
tendant upon the official recognition would be harmful, since there
is no way to give public credit without also mentioning the record
of deviation. This is presumably why, as Scheff's account (43) so
clearly shows, we would find it anomalous to see public pronounce-

---

* Some of these problems are discussed in the context of penal sanctions by
Joseph Goldstein in "Police Discretion Not to Invoke the Criminal Process:
Low Visibility Decisions in the Administration of Justice," *Yale Law Journal*,
Vol. 69, 1960.

ments calling attention to a person's former status as a mental patient, except when further deviant behavior occurs. There is asymmetry in the process similar to that noted in the development of knowledge about the recruit.

Finally, re-entry is likely to operate differently in the two cases because of differences in the general "set" of the new social environments into which the former recruits will be moving. Because passage through developmental organizations is expected and routine, the organizations into which the former recruits pass have worked out standard modes of organizing the transition. Hiring policies, for example, are often predicated on the routine entry of persons into the labor force in June, when graduation occurs.

Because those leaving resocialization settings have been in a different sort of career cycle and because they are typically a small proportion of all new entrants, they present problems for the receiving organization quite unlike those presented by others. These are problems in addition to whatever problems of stigma may arise from their having been defined as in need of resocialization. Since they have been sidetracked, the recruits are frequently re-entering a setting most of their peers passed through earlier. A good example is the return of a juvenile offender from a youth institution. He may be returning to the ninth grade although old enough for the eleventh and may suffer the further embarrassment of finding a younger sibling in the same class. Whatever agents in the organization may feel about him, he is above all a special case for which there may not be a clear policy. He moves from being one of many, and so regarded by agents in the resocialization setting, to being one of very few in his new setting. Routine processing procedures are likely to be lacking, and the former recruit may sense quite accurately that he is making trouble wherever he goes.

Organizational Control and the Recruit's Later Career

Immediate problems of exit from organizations are more visible but probably less important than the nature of the long-term tie between the organization and its former recruits. Some of those who have passed through may have no further ties with the organization once they have left, and others may have extensive ties. But since the recruit, by definition, is being prepared in some sense for participation outside the organization, there are likely to be ties that provide a linkage between the organization and the recruit's later career.

Clearly, an important informal tie is the status of the organization in the eyes of the community. Over time, the nature of the recruit's specific participation in the organization may become less important than the fact that he participated at all. This appears especially true of the most prestigeful and the most notorious settings, those that are likely to be most firmly embedded in the public mind. Some doors will be open to those who have graduated from elite colleges irrespective of their performance, and some will be closed to ex-prison inmates even though they have established stellar records as inmates. Thus, wherever the individual's reputation is at stake, his past membership identities become critical reference points, quite apart from his specific accomplishments or misdeeds while in the organization. It is only organizations that are invisible, bland, or neutral, or those where membership can be concealed, that have no link to a later career.

There are often more formal linkages than those established by the reputation of organizations and hence to some extent of their participants. Some organizations that process people also control entry to the careers for which the people are being prepared. They not only socialize their recruits; they also are responsible for placing them in specific positions. They may have to certify that the individual is properly trained and therefore deserving of the license; less formally they may write recommendations for him, describing his relevant attributes. Wherever the organization has the power to determine the recruit's fate after he leaves it, it has an added means of social control over him while he is being socialized.

Where this is the case, a strain is likely to exist between the individual's ability to meet the formal qualifications as laid out in examinations, courses of study, and other requirements, and his ability to meet the unstated, informal qualifications actually employed by those who provide access to positions outside the socialization system. The degree of identity or discrepancy between these two sets of requirements probably varies widely across different types of socialization environments.

Indeed, some might prefer to restrict the term socialization to this latter, informal preparation, regarding the formal portion as mere training. In some situations, the formal part can be learned with little participation. This is true, for example, of much advanced academic work where access to a good library may be more important than formal enrollment in courses. It is precisely the personal and informal side that cannot be presumed in this way.

One might think of a simple typology of modes of exit from organizations, depending upon whether the person leaving has both the formal and the informal qualifications, one or the other, or neither. It seems likely that socializing organizations will differ in the extent to which their recruits leave with these various properties. This seems to be undoubtedly one of the consequences of differences in size and scale of socializing organizations. Familiar examples are the senior at a large university who has outstanding, specialized training but is almost unknown to the faculty, and his counterpart at a smaller college who has been informally socialized by the teaching staff but whose formal training may have suffered because of the lack of a rich and varied program. The point is that these obvious and familiar differences do not merely produce different types of recruit; they also forge different linkages with the recruit's later career, in one case the linkage coming primarily through the formal bureaucratic system, in the other through informal interpersonal networks. The distinction is not necessarily the recruit's choice; it depends in important ways on the structure of the organization through which he is passing.

Socialization Chains and Sequences

Often the total process of socialization is organized into separate environments that are linked in a sequence, thus producing additional problems of movement from one to another. Such sequences are of course built into the educational system, with transitions from primary to junior to senior high school, through the colleges and graduate schools. There is often a parallel sequence in movement through resocialization organizations and many other similar age-graded sequences.*

These sequences are frequently highly collapsed in time with

* (It is interesting to note that schools and prisons are probably most alike at the earliest stage. From then on, movement up in one sequence brings increasing freedom and self-direction, whereas movement up the other may have the reverse consequences, especially when judged against similar age grades outside the setting. This condition lies at the heart of the immense feeling of powerlessness and lack of self-determination experienced by many men in prison.)

rapid transition from one to another. An example is the series of developments that precede hospitalization for mental illness and their function in the socialization of persons into the role of mental patient (28). It is not surprising that these rapid transitional stages are more often associated with remedial and resocialization organizations than with developmental ones, for they frequently involve problematic and unplanned events. A parallel sequence in another realm of deviant behavior is the movement of delinquents and criminals from police, through the courts, and into correctional establishments.

The agents who arrange such a sequence have a number of interesting properties. They are spatially separated and frequently do not know each other and are likely to come from varying social and occupational careers and hence to have different images of their tasks. Also, each works within a different organization that presents demands of its own. All these features add up to an enormous potential for the presentation of conflicting images of the total sequence to the person moving through it. Consider, for example, the range of views about his problems a delinquent may receive from police, probation officers, judges, psychiatrists, and correctional officials, all of whom may have a hand in his movement through the sequence.

In addition to these sources of confusion and ambiguity, there is likely to be a strong bias in the presentation of each agent to make the next stage appear benign. This is so because the agent at one stage has to establish working relations with the person while he is in that stage, and will find that he is more cooperative if he thinks things look bright for the future. If a severe action must be taken, there may be an attempt to minimize its severity. By the time the person has moved through the full sequence, it is not surprising that he has a large residue of mistrust. The outstanding case is the "betrayal funnel," Goffman's phrase for the pattern of deceit involved in commitments to mental hospitals.

A related feature is that the only persons who have moved through the whole sequence are the *targets* of resocialization, and not the agents. Thus the best possible source of information on the process as a whole is another person who has gone through it, has failed, and is going through it again. In a panel study of boys moving from a reception and diagnostic unit to one of five or six institutions for delinquents, we are finding that the only effective sources of information about the institutions during the time a boy is in the diagnostic unit are other boys who have been there and are starting through again. It is not simply that the boys prefer to look to their peers. They *have* to look to their peers because the staff at the diagnostic center knows little about the new organizations, which are many miles away.

Finally, whenever there are sequences of socialization environments, we find what might be called the "fish and pond" problems. The oldest junior high school class becomes the youngest group in high school and must readjust to its relative standing; the boy who had a poor reputation in a small town finds that in youth institutions he is an angel compared to some of the big city recruits. Wherever age of entry is some measure of precocity, we may find that the usual age-graded status patterns are reversed. A youth has to be exceptionally bad by the standards of the official system to be committed to a reformatory for young adults at age 17, but he may have to be good to be committed there, instead of to an adult penitentiary, at age 26. Because of these reversals, the stereotype of the youthful, naive inmate being criminally influenced by the older, more mature prisoner is frequently quite false.

ORGANIZATION AND SOCIETY

Like other organizations, those that process people are embedded in a broader social system that helps shape its goals, provides both agents and recruits, and supplies the material resources that sustain it. Furthermore, the success or failure of socializing organizations depends heavily on the fate of their recruits after they have returned to the broader system. A thorough review of the relations between such organizations and the external world is neither feasible nor necessary here, since many of the features are found as well in other types of formal organization. But it does seem relevant to discuss several features that specifically affect the operations of organizations that process people.

Organizational Change and Personal Change

So far, socialization environments have been discussed as though they were static and constant. Only the individuals moving through them are presumed to be changing. Of course the settings change as well, and some fascinating substantive problems emerge when the personal change takes place within a changing organizational framework.

A critical question is the following: under what circumstances will personal and organizational change be *congruent* in their effects on socialization, and when *incongruent?* We would regard them as congruent where both personal development and organizational development are moving in the same direction over time, incongruent where they are moving in opposite directions. Where they are incongruent, we may expect one element to at least partially cancel the other, so that the total change is smaller than might otherwise be expected.

An example of incongruence is found in the historical development of correctional philosophy and ideology. The strong trend has been toward a more liberal and humanizing view. But from various opinion and personality studies where age is used as a variable, it appears that personal change is in the opposite direction. People become more conservative, perhaps more punitive and authoritarian, as they move further into adulthood and middle age. Stouffer's study (47) of the effects of age on attitudes toward communism provides one good illustration of this effect. In the prison setting, guards who have remained in their jobs for a long time are pulled one way by organizational change and the opposite way, possibly, by age-related personality changes. At least one study reports no sizable relationship between either chronological age or length of time in the system and authoritarianism, for the custodial staff of a large prison system (35). This finding may be a result of the canceling effect of personal change on one hand and organizational change on the other. Another example is found in schools, where the older a teacher becomes, the more likely she is to be exposed to more modern and progressive methods.

It is rare to have adequate data on such processes. Measurement on individuals and on organizations over long periods of time is required. Problems of organizational and personal change are fascinating enough, however, to warrant this extra investment of time and energy.

The Organization and External Interest Groups

The ties of recruits to the external system have already been discussed. Equally important are the external groups that apply pressure on the organization as a whole and thus serve to influence its policies and programs. Administrators are often under pressure from a variety of external groups who have economic or other forms of investment in the organization. Some organizations are also surrounded by voluntary associations or other types of institution whose members are generally concerned with its progress as a whole and specifically with the welfare of the recruit population. Where such groups exist, they may intervene on behalf of the recruits and form powerful pressure groups to express their interests.

Such groups are typically stronger and more influential in the developmental socialization settings. Persons who formerly occupied the status of recruit often retain an interest in organization and are the logical members of the external interest groups. Typically, the greater the prestige or desirability of the organization to its recruits, the greater their later commitment and interest in it. Their interest, however, is not an unmixed blessing for agents. These external interest groups may be used to help raise funds, support controversial policies, and so forth; but because their situation no longer includes being members of the recruit population, their perspectives on the organization and its purposes may change. A specific problem is that members of external groups often judge the organization by matters that are most visible to outsiders and not by the daily run of internal events. In schools and colleges, interscholastic athletic performance and competition, the presence of noted lecturers, or artistic performances by bands, choirs, or other groups are likely to be the most visible signs of activity. Changes in the physical structure, such as new buildings or parks, are also likely to be noted. Less obvious are the daily internal operations such as the quality of teaching, or the relations between teacher and student, although these may be more critical in achieving the major goals of the organization. The dimension is that of the visibility of the organization, and various parts of it, to the external world.

Representatives of resocialization settings receive both the benefits and the liabilities that come from having relatively weaker outside interest groups concerned with the welfare of their recruits. Unlike the former recruits of developmental organizations, those from resocialization settings are not likely to be proud of their previous membership or of the organization and therefore less frequently show an interest in the setting after leaving. Also, they are probably less influential in the social order, because of their prior official histories as deviants. Thus in resocialization settings there is likely to be no equivalent to such activities as alumni pressure to support the football team or to fire faculty members with questionable political beliefs (though where recruits are less often drawn from the lower reaches of society, for example, private mental hospitals, relatives may fill this role). Perhaps the closest equivalent to such groups in many resocializing organizations is provided by the mass media. Newspaper exposés of conditions on the back wards and the frequency with which inmates require the presence of a favored journalist when negotiating a truce with the staff after a prison riot indicate the importance of this function.

Since organizations that process people are often supported by public funds, the nature of the governmental systems within which they operate becomes an important determinant of life within them. There is a vast difference, for example, between the orientation of many administrators of American prisons and that of their Scandinavian counterparts. Scandinavian administrators, their prisons being less subject to the immediate pressures of government, are able to take a longer-range view of the development of their systems. American administrators appear to be more crisis oriented, since prison conditions often become foci of public attention during election campaigns, and state governors and other officials have good reason to want to keep prisons running quietly. These differing conceptions of time and critical events are likely to ramify through the organizations, having a substantial but perhaps indirect impact upon the recruits.

Evaluation of Organizational Outcomes

Like any other organization that produces something, organizations whose products are people face evaluative tasks. Precisely because the product is human, however, there are imponderables in the process of evaluation that seem to exceed those of most industries. The difficulties arise both in comparing individual recruits within a given establishment and in comparing outcomes from the organization as a whole with those from others of its kind.

Evaluation must be geared to the organization's goals, and to the extent that it is difficult to establish and agree upon the goals, evaluation of outcomes is impossible. Even if there is agreement on the goals, evaluation is beset by other problems. If the training takes a long time, changes in the person being trained may be indicative of maturational shifts rather than the effects of the organization. Where larger social changes are occurring outside the socialization organization, shifts in the persons being socialized may be brought about by the external society rather than by the organization itself. Jacob (33) noted, for example, that changes in college student attitudes and values often mirrored the changes occurring more generally in society, and questioned whether these shifts should be thought of as attributable to the college itself.

When different organizations are to be compared, there must clearly be some control for input into the systems. Colleges may produce a large number of Ph.D.'s because they get Ph.D. material; prisons may have low rates of parole failure among their former recruits because they receive only the best risks. The importance of differential input is so great that any appropriate evaluation across organizations must contain efforts to control for differences in input.

The problem does not end with controlling the input of recruits. Suppose that two colleges, "Brightsville" and "Dullsville," could be shown to produce similar outcomes, controlling for differences in the average intelligence of student input. The two are probably not equivalent in the range of abilities, interests, and commitments of their staffs, so it would be inappropriate to suppose that there is no effect because of the nature of the organizations and the composition of its socializing agents. Rather, there may be an interaction effect: it may take a more specialized staff to produce the same amount of change in the bright students that is produced in the dull ones. Were we simply to exchange the student populations from one institution to the other, we would expect sizable differences in the relative amounts of change among the students, or compensating shifts in the interests and abilities of staff members. Each may have either a heightening or a lowering effect on the output of the other; the full evaluation design will have to include the qualities of both agent and recruit.

Finally, since socializing organizations are designed to prepare their recruits for roles outside the organization, there is an acute problem of feedback in the measurement of outcomes. It may take several years of follow-up before one can reasonably decide whether the person is a successful product. Studies of the effects that stop at showing changes in attitudes among recruits during the length of stay but give no evidence about later behavior typically beg all sorts of questions about the relation of attitudinal or behavioral change while in the organization to behavior after getting out. The practical effectiveness of group therapy, for example, depends on whether those who receive it come back to prisons and mental hospitals less often than similar types of inmates or patients who do not receive it. That they feel better, verbalize differently, or even are more comfortable during their stay would not typically be taken as evidence of the program's success, unless they also do better after leaving.

The reason for stressing all these problems of evaluation is not solely to reiterate the well-known difficulties of conducting evaluation studies of these types of organization. The technical problems are well known by those who have attempted such studies (3); indeed it is possible to exaggerate the problems. Comparative studies of the impact of school and college training are being carried out, and there are the beginnings of systematic evaluation research on resocializing organizations, such as the studies now being conducted within the California correctional system (8). But the major point is that most socializing organizations must operate in the absence of data that bear in a pertinent way on the effectiveness of their programs. The lack of such data appears to have at least two important effects upon the experiences to which the recruit population is exposed.

First, there is a natural tendency to utilize any conveniently measurable variable as a possible "impact" measure, with the result that the presumed means to socialization goals may become elevated to ends in themselves. Perhaps the most familiar instance is the use of quantitative measures of written productivity as indicators of the quality of a university faculty. Certainly one reason for the use of such a measure is that research productivity is important in an academic community. But perhaps another reason is that the quantity is there to be counted, whereas measures of the quality of the professor's contribution to the training of students are less easily developed. In resocialization organizations, we often find implicit evaluations of their quality based upon such indirect measures as the staff-inmate ratio, the proportion of all staff that are professionals, or the presence of specific programs that meet standards set by professional agencies. The import of these modes of evaluation for recruits is simply that the major ostensible goals of the organization may become deflected because of the use of incomplete or inappropriate but available evaluation measures.

The second problem is that, where evaluation is difficult, the doors are open for highly competing views of appropriate socialization programs. Organization staff may be left with a haunting uncertainty about the relevance of their current actions for the future careers of the recruits. Since flaws can be found in any evaluation effort, it may be difficult to establish legitimate grounds for criticism of programs. Determination of policy will then depend much more on the relative power of various interest groups than on evidence about the program's effectiveness. The functions of such weaknesses in evaluation research for correctional institutions have been pointed out by Cressey (18).

Thus, to the extent that meaningful evaluation of programs and outcomes is difficult, the actual effect of programs on recruits will remain unknown, and there will be no clearly established linkage between programs and outcomes. Under such conditions, there is less probability that the programs are actually meeting the intended purposes of the socialization organization. Important areas for further research are determining the variations across organizations in the extent to which they provide clear measurement of outcomes of their programs, and the ways in which modes of evaluation affect the actual circumstances to which recruits are exposed.

The Balance between Socialization and Social Control

Throughout this work the existence of organizations devoted both to socialization and to resocialization or social control has been taken for granted. It has been assumed that there is a flow of persons moving into each type and that the organizations exist to receive them. But one of the most fascinating and also most important of problems has to do precisely with the existence of both types of setting and specifically of the balance between them. There is no hard and fast level at which we distinguish the bright from the stupid, the well from the sick, the good from the bad. There is no binding rule that demands equal support of both genius and retarded, saint and sinner. These matters are socially determined.

We can inquire, then, across societies or through one society at different points in time, into the relative amount of support provided for advancing the skills of those already defined as conventional, versus the amount devoted to rebuilding the skills of the deviant. For example, we can consider the ratio of expenses for prisons and mental hospitals to those for educational facilities. Or, within the category of education, consider expenses for the training of the gifted versus those for the retarded. Apart from how far financial and human resources are devoted to one or another of these categories, we can consider the number of persons singled out as belonging to one or another of these groups, and possible changes in that number over time or place. We can ask what the conditions are under which a society will become especially sensitive to the needs of its needy, or the talents of its talented. For the category of deviants in need of resocialization, when will its resources favor the criminal and when the sick?

Questions such as these move our focus from the problems of socialization settings, agents, and recruits to the processes by which agent, recruit, and setting are constructed. What began as a personal problem for persons being socialized has become a societal problem of the allocation of its human and material resources.

Answers to these questions are not likely to come easily, for the problems require analysis of the flow of power and decision-making within and between local, state, and national jurisdictions. Yet a sharp focus on such problems seems essential if we are to understand where and how our socializing organizations fit into the broader social structure. It seems clear that it is precisely the nature of this fit between the organization and the broader system that is crucially relevant, in the long run, for the fates of those who pass through them.

CONCLUSION

There is really no appropriate and logical end to a list of the properties or socializing organizations that may influence socialization outcomes. At least at this point in organization theory, questions of the distinctive relevance or the explanatory power of various dimensions are just beginning to be answered with empirical data. An arbitrary limitation was imposed by the choice of only a few from the nearly infinite list of organizational dimensions that could conceivably influence socialization outcomes. Aside from those that are clearly found only in organizations that process people, the criterion for inclusion in each case was the seemingly greater importance of the dimension in socializing organizations than in other organizational settings.

Little has been said, for example, about the extent of the human or material resources available to an organization or about the degree to which it operates as an autonomous unit or as part of a broader system. In some instances, such as the junior college case examined in detail by Clark (14), a variable like dependency on a broader district looms as critical. It was not analyzed here because such a feature is clearly not limited to socialization settings; any formal organization has some degree of dependence on or autonomy from its surrounding environment. But another one of the aspects of Clark's analysis is highly germane, namely, the extent to which members of the setting can control the selection of their recruits.

One of the crucial omissions in the present work, and seemingly an important problem for further research, is how specific interactions between socializing agent and recruit depend upon variations in the broader organizational setting. It seems quite reasonable to suppose that the way in which any person treats another whom he is ostensibly training depends on the nature of his own relationship with the broader organization in which he is embedded. What the psychiatrist tells his patient, the guard his inmate, the teacher his student, will vary in systematic ways with the character of the organizations to which they are attached. An essential limitation of the present essay is that it does not specify these linkages in detail. Instead the focus has been on the organization itself and not on the direct interchange between agent and recruit.

A further omission, related to both the nature of resources and the interaction between agent and recruit, concerns the technology by which socialization agencies attempt to accomplish their task. A fine-grained comparison of the ways in which "people-work" is accomplished may tell us much about the potential effects of alternative techniques. Such an analysis would require a detailed treatment of the styles of communication used in different socialization efforts as well as analysis of the more obvious technological features of socialization settings such as the use of audio-visual aids or "team" teaching efforts.

Still another problem is that the nature of the dependent variable, namely, some type of socialization outcome, has been left quite unspecified in this work. The relatively meager amount of research actually devoted to the effects of various socialization settings provides one reason for the lack of specificity. But it should be clear that the conditions are likely to be related in varying ways to differing types of outcome. Whether the changes that take place are long-lasting, whether they concern attitudes or overt behavior, or indeed whether they take place at all in response to formally organized settings, are questions that largely remain to be answered.

The need for further descriptive and comparative research seems abundantly clear. There are many case studies of single organizations, using either observational or survey research methods, and a handful of studies compare a number of different organizations with regard to their formal qualities and socialization outcomes. Thus we have Coleman's study of schools (16), Vinter, Janowitz, and others' reports on correctional facilities for youths (49), and the work by Clark and Trow on student subcultures (15). But such studies are just beginning, and they tend to accentuate what goes on in the largest and most visible socializing organizations, such as high schools and colleges, medical schools, and prisons. Although the great variety of trade schools may be numerically less important in the total numbers of persons they process, analytically they are a strategic locus for studies of socialization processes and outcomes, and much should be learned from research on such settings.* In any

* To my knowledge, the most extensive study of that sort is the one now being carried out by Howard S. Becker and Blanche Geer. Personal communications from them suggest that some of the propositions in this essay will need modification if they are to apply as well to the wide variety of trade schools.

event, what seems clear is that we are just beginning to spell out the important ways that socialization settings can vary and thus can lead to radically different outcomes for their recruits.

The chief problem posed by a long list of variables is to determine what it is good for. Endless distinctions can be drawn and occasional insights may be found, but if the variables reviewed above are to be really useful, they must enter into propositions that explain something. Variations in the structure of socialization settings must be shown to be linked systematically to variations in socialization outcomes.

An attempt has been made to introduce at least a partial linkage by comparing developmental socialization settings with resocialization settings. One conclusion is that even the best-managed and best-designed centers for the resocialization of deviants operate under organizational handicaps less frequently found in developmental settings. Their lesser power of selection of recruits, their lesser time to prepare for the recruits' entrance into programs, their requirement to keep failures rather than successes, their lesser support from interested parties outside the organization, their typically greater conflict and disagreement about goals, and a number of the other dimensions which have been discussed suggest that resocialization settings are less suited than developmental settings for producing lasting changes in attitudes, values, and behavior that go in the direction desired by the socializing agents. When these differences are coupled with differences in the motivations and abilities of individual recruits, the problems facing resocialization settings emerge sharply.

Even this type of conclusion must remain highly tentative, however, for there are no current methods for testing hypotheses regarding differential outcomes from such diverse types of setting. The few studies that provide data on a large enough number of organizations to say something about the effects of different types of settings typically draw their material from only one of the range of types. In order to test adequately the above claims regarding differences in developmental and resocialization settings, criteria of successful and unsuccessful outcomes must be established that are broad enough to encompass all these types of setting. But how well must a prison do in order to be achieving the same success in socialization outcome as, say, a grammar school, a university, or a barber college? Since the units for the measurement of success are not comparable across the settings, claims regarding differential effectiveness must be resolved largely by debate rather than evidence.

Cumulative evidence regarding the effectiveness of socialization settings is likely to come, therefore, from studies in which organizations of similar general type are compared. And of course a complete picture of the variables that produce different socialization outcomes will include those that operate at the individual level. Indeed, a scheme for the organization of relevant data is suggested by borrowing from the study of individual role learning. Brim (13) has proposed that any variable affecting individual differences in the learning of social roles does so through one of three intervening processes. The independent variable must affect either (a) the individual's awareness and knowledge of the norms and role demands being placed upon him, (b) his ability to deliver the required performance, or (c) his motivation to do so. In brief, where the personal or environmental variable has an effect, it must operate by affecting the individual's knowledge, his ability to perform, or his motivation.

If the dimensions of socialization settings described in this paper have an effect on socialization outcomes, that effect is probably mediated through a parallel set of intervening processes. The conditions may operate to change (a) the organization's capacity to provide clear and unambiguous norms for performance, (b) its capacity to provide opportunities for learning and practicing the required performance, or (c) its capacity to selectively reward the behavior of its recruits. Most of the dimensions which have been described appear to be linked to one or more of these intervening processes.

The organization's capacity to provide clear and unambiguous norms for its recruits obviously depends to some extent on the degree of consensus in goals. It also depends upon at least a minimal amount of time for interaction with the recruits in order to communicate effectively what the norms are. Furthermore, though less obvious, it depends on the absence of contrary definitions of the norms that might be espoused by others in positions to influence the recruit, such as his peers. The organization may be able to provide clearer norms for some of its members than for others, depending on their location in the formal and informal structure of the organization and on their rate of interaction with socializing agents. For example, if recruits that do not support the organization's norms are more visible to other recruits than are those who do support the norms, there may be a basis for lack of clear communication of the relevant norms (52).

The organization's capacity to provide relevant learning and performance opportunities depends partly on how long before entry it has an opportunity to influence the recruit (so that he may learn some parts of the required performance before actual participation in the setting), its capacity to assign him to the programs most relevant for him (which depends upon knowledge about his prior performances), the number of minutes, weeks, hours, or days he can spend in close interaction with those who can teach him the required performance, and the extent of external support provided by the organization.

The organization's capacity to selectively reward its recruits clearly depends on the structure of its relations to the external community, including the extent of its power to place the recruit in positions for which his training prepares him. The organization's capacity to reward the recruit will also depend upon the nature of its resources, including its power to provide status, prestige, money, or other valued items in return for acceptable performance. And the ability to selectively reward recruits, as well as the capacity to teach them the norms and required performances, clearly depends on the quality of the socializing agents brought into the organization.

The full framework would be as illustrated in the diagram on p. 112. The independent variables may be either individual or organizational characteristics. If they have an impact on socialization outcomes, they do so through some combination of the three intervening processes reflecting, respectively, the norms governing the system, the specific behavior patterns to be learned, and the structure of reward or motivation to learn. Both individual and organization may, of course be affected by elements of the broader social context, and the socialization problems faced in any one setting may not equally entail all three intervening processes. An adequate sociological theory of socialization outcomes will require specification of the most relevant independent variables, their linkages through the intervening processes to varying socialization outcomes, and the conditions under which such patterns hold.

Framework for Analysis of Socialization in Organizations

		Intervening Mechanisms		
		Organizational	Individual	
	Norms	Capacity to present clear norms	Capacity to learn the norms	Sociali-zation Outcomes
Inde-pendent → Variables	Performances	Capacity to provide performance oppor-tunities	Capacity to perform	
	Rewards, Sanctions, Motives	Capacity to selectively reward performance	Motivation to perform	

Application of this simple scheme to the analysis of aggregate outcomes in socialization settings would thus require locating the setting using indicators of six dimensions, three at the organizational level and three representing the input from the recruits. One would expect the most favorable socialization outcomes, from the point of view of the socializing agency, in settings where the typical recruit is motivated and capable of learning both the norms and the required performances, and where the setting itself presents a clear normative structure, offers many opportunities for performance, and has the power of selective reward. But in many cases the joint impact of individual and organizational variables may take other than an additive form. Also, many of the interesting cases may occur where individual and organizational forces tend to be opposed—when relatively mediocre students confront an excellent faculty, very good students a mediocre faculty, and so on.

This same scheme may be applied to individuals within differing socialization settings. Here one might anticipate important contextual effects; effects on the reform-oriented inmate in a prison where most inmates are opposed to the staff, the bright and motivated student in the school where many are dull and unmotivated, and so forth. Models for the analysis of such circumstances have been provided by Blau (11), Barton (2), Davis (19), and others. They seem well suited to capture some of the rich possibilities of different socialization outcomes under varying individual and organizational conditions.

Perhaps the chief question remaining concerns the long-term impact of organizations as socialization agencies. Now that we have defined a category of organizations wherein socialization is supposed to take place, our attention has been drawn to probable differentials in effectiveness. It may well be that organizations designed to create lasting personal change are not the ideal mechanisms. It seems possible that the modal response among recruits to all such settings is outward compliance with the aims and goals of the setting, coupled with a variety of secondary adjustments differing in form, strength, and character, depending on the individual's personal needs, his particular position in the socialization setting, and the nature and strength of his attachments outside it. The opposite assumption, namely, that such organizations have great impact and that there are sizable differentials between them, clearly underlies the discussion in this essay. But the lack of really good evidence justifying either assumption requires a tentative tone throughout.

We can be sure, however, that organizations whose products are people will play an increasingly significant role in modern societies. As formal organizations they provide an important reference point for the study of other types of bureaucratic structure. As socialization settings they may have much impact on the later careers of those who pass through them. Detailed study of their forms and consequences would appear to be a strategically important task for social science.

Bibliography

1. Asch, Solomon, "Effects of Group Pressure upon the Modification and Distortion of Judgment," *Groups, Leadership and Men*, Edited by H. Guetz Kow, Pittsburgh: The Carnegie Press, 1951.
2. Barton, Allen H., *Organizational Measurement*, New York: College Entrance Examination Board, 1961.
3. Barton, Allen H., *Studying the Effects of College Education, A Methodological Examination of Changing Values in College*, New Haven, Connecticut: The Edward W. Hazen Foundation, 1959.
4. Becker, Howard S., "Personal Change in Adult Life," *Sociometry*, Vol. 27, No. 1, March, 1964, pp. 40–53.

5. Becker, Howard S., and Blanche Geer, "Fate of Idealism in Medical School," *American Sociological Review*, Vol. 23, No. 1, February, 1958, pp. 50–56.
6. Becker, Howard S., and Blanche Geer, "Latent Culture: A Note on the Theory of Latent Social Roles," *Administrative Science Quarterly*, Vol. 5, No. 2, September, 1960, pp. 304–313.
7. Becker, Howard S., and Blanche Geer, "Student Culture in Medical School," *Harvard Educational Review*, Vol. 28, No. 1, Winter, 1958, pp. 70–80.
8. Beverly, Robert F., *Base Expectancies and the Initial Home Visit Research Schedule*, Research Report Number 37, State of California, Youth and Adult Corrections Agency, Department of the Youth Authority, Division of Research, January, 1964.
9. Bidwell, Charles E., "Pre-Adult Socialization," a paper presented at the Social Science Research Council Conference on Socialization and Social Structure, May, 1962.
10. Bidwell, Charles E., and Rebecca S. Vreeland, "College Education and Moral Orientations: An Organizational Approach," presented at the annual meeting of the American Sociological Association, August 30, 1962.
11. Blau, Peter M., "Structural Effects," *American Sociological Review*, Vol. 25, 1960, pp. 178–199.
12. Blau, Peter, and W. Richard Scott, *Formal Organizations*, San Francisco: Chandler Publishing Company, 1962.
13. Brim, Orville G., Jr., "Personality Development as Role-Learning," in *Personality Development in Children*, Edited by Ira Iscoe and Harold Stevenson, Austin: University of Texas Press, 1960, pp. 127–159.
14. Clark, Burton R., *The Open-Door College: A Case Study*, New York: McGraw-Hill, 1960.
15. Clark, Burton R., and Martin Trow, "Determinants of College Student Sub-cultures," unpublished manuscript.
16. Coleman, James S., *Adolescent Society*, Glencoe, Illinois: The Free Press.
17. Cressey, Donald R., "Limitations on Organization of Treatment in the Modern Prison," in *Theoretical Studies in the Social Organization of the Prison*, Edited by Richard A. Cloward *et al.*, New York: Social Science Research Council, 1960, pp. 78–110.
18. Cressey, Donald R., "The Nature and Effectiveness of Correctional Techniques," *The National Probation and Parole Association Journal*, 1960.
19. Davis, James A., *Great Books and Small Groups*, Glencoe, Illinois: The Free Press, 1962, Chapter 1.
20. Dornbusch, Sanford M., "The Military Academy as an Assimilating Institution," *Social Forces*, Vol. XXXIII, 1955, p. 317.

21. Etzioni, Amitai, *A Comparative Analysis of Complex Organizations*, Glencoe, Illinois: The Free Press, 1961.
22. Garabedian, Peter C., "Social Roles and Processes of Socialization in the Prison Community," *Social Problems*, Vol. 11, Fall, 1963, pp. 139–152.
23. Garfinkel, Harold, "Conditions of Successful Degradation Ceremonies," *American Journal of Sociology*, Vol. LXI, 1956, pp. 420–424.
24. Garrity, Donald L., "The Effect of Length of Incarceration upon Parole Adjustment and Estimation of Optimum Sentences; Washington State Correctional Institution," unpublished Ph.D. Thesis, 1956.
25. Giallombardo, Rose, *The Social Structure of a Women's Prison*, unpublished Ph.D. Dissertation, Northwestern University, Evanston, Illinois, 1965.
26. Gibbons, Don C., *Changing the Law-Breaker*, Englewood Cliffs, New Jersey: Prentice-Hall, 1964.
27. Goffman, Erving, "The Moral Career of the Mental Patient," *Asylums*, Garden City, New York: Anchor Books, Doubleday, 1961, pp. 125–169.
28. Goffman, Erving, "On the Characteristics of Total Institutions," *Asylums*, Garden City, New York: Anchor Books, Doubleday, 1961, pp. 1–124.
29. Goldstein, Joseph, "Police Discretion Not to Invoke the Criminal Process: Low Visibility Decisions in the Administration of Justice," *Yale Law Journal*, Vol. 69, 1960.
30. Gouldner, Alvin, *Patterns of Industrial Bureaucracy*, Glencoe, Illinois: The Free Press, 1954.
31. Hughes, Everett C., *Men and Their Work*, Glencoe, Illinois: The Free Press, 1958, p. 76.
32. Irwin, John, and Donald R. Cressey, "Thieves, Convicts, and the Inmate Culture," *Social Problems*, Vol. 10, Fall, 1962.
33. Jacob, Philip E., *Changing Values in College*, New York: Harper, 1957.
34. Jones, Maxwell, *The Therapeutic Community*, New York: Basic Books, Inc., 1953.
35. Kassebaum, Gene G., David A. Ward, Daniel M. Wilner, and Will C. Kennedy, "Job Related Differences in Staff Attitudes toward Treatment in a Women's Prison," *Pacific Sociological Review*, Vol. 5, No. 2, Fall, 1962, pp. 83–88.
36. Klapp, Orin, *Heroes, Villains, and Fools*, Glencoe, Illinois: The Free Press, 1963.
37. Lippitt, R., and R. K. White, "An Experimental Study of Leadership and Group Life," in *Readings in Social Psychology*, Edited by G. E. Swanson, T. M. Newcomb, and G. L. Hartley, New York: Henry Holt, 1952.

38. Maccoby, Eleanor, "The Choice of Variables in the Study of Socialization," *Sociometry*, Vol. 24, No. 4, December, 1961.
39. McHugh, Peter, paper delivered at the American Sociological Association meetings, 1964.
40. Parsons, Talcott, "An Approach to Psychological Theory in Terms of the Theory of Action," in *Psychology: A Study of a Science*, Edited by Sigmund Koch, New York: McGraw-Hill, Vol. III, 1959.
41. Parsons, Talcott, "Suggestions for a Sociological Approach to the Theory of Organizations, I, II," *Administrative Science Quarterly*, Vol. 1, 1956, pp. 63–85 and 225–239.
42. Roth, Julius A., "The Timetable in Treatment and in Everyday Life," unpublished paper for the Committee on Human Development, University of Chicago, Chicago, Illinois, January, 1959.
43. Scheff, Thomas J., "The Role of the Mentally Ill and the Dynamics of Mental Disorder: A Research Framework," *Sociometry*, Vol. 26, No. 4, December, 1963.
44. Schrag, Clarence, "A Preliminary Criminal Typology," *Pacific Sociological Review*, Vol. 4, No. 1, Spring, 1961, pp. 11–16.
45. Sewell, William H., "Some Recent Developments in Socialization Theory and Research," in *The Annals of the American Academy of Political and Social Science*, Philadelphia, Vol. 349, September, 1963, pp. 163–181.
46. Shils, Edward, "Primary Groups in the Modern Army," in *Continuities in Social Research; Studies in the Scope and Method of the Modern Soldier*, Edited by Robert K. Merton and Paul F. Lazarsfeld, Glencoe, Illinois: The Free Press, 1953.
47. Stouffer, Samuel A., *Communism, Conformity, and Civil Liberties*, Garden City, New York: Doubleday, 1955.
48. Sykes, Gresham M., *The Society of Captives*, Princeton, New Jersey: Princeton University Press, 1958.
49. Vinter, Robert, and Morris Janowitz, "Effective Institutions for Juvenile Offenders: A Research Statement," *Social Service Review*, Vol. 33, June, 1959, pp. 118–131.
50. Wallace, Walter L., "Institutional and Life-Cycle Socialization of College Freshmen," *American Journal of Sociology*, Vol. LXX, No. 3, November, 1964.
51. Wheeler, Stanton, "Socialization in Correctional Communities," *American Sociological Review*, Vol. XXVI, October, 1961, pp. 699–712.
52. Wheeler, Stanton, "Role Conflict in Correctional Communities," in *The Prison: Studies in Institutional Organization and Change*, Edited by Donald R. Cressey, New York: Holt-Rinehart-Winston, 1961, Chapter 6.